MYSTICAL
SEX

MYSTICAL
SEX

Love, Ecstasy, and
the Mystical Experience

LOUIS WILLIAM MELDMAN, Ph.D.

Harbinger House
Tucson • *New York*

HARBINGER HOUSE, INC.
Tucson, Arizona

∞ This book was printed on acid-free, archival-quality paper
Typeset in 11/14 Zapf International Light
Designed by Walser Design
Illustrations by Theresa Smith

Figure 1 on page 49 is an artist's rendering of an illustration from "Rosarium philosophorum," a sixteenth-century manuscript of Kantonsbibliothek (Vadiana) in St. Gallen, Switzerland.

Library of Congress Cataloging-in-Publication Data

Meldman, Louis William, 1952–
Mystical sex : love, ecstasy, and the mystical experience /
Louis William Meldman.
p.   cm.
Includes bibliographical references (p.
ISBN 0-943173-70-1 (alk. paper) : $9.95
1. Sex.   2. Sex (psychology)   3. Mysticism.   I. Title.
HQ19.M46   1990
306.7—dc20   90-33641

Contents

Contents

Introduction

Moving Past Medical Dogma Toward a Meaningful, Higher Understanding of Sex

---

For perhaps three-quarters of all males, orgasm is reached within two minutes after the initiation of sexual relations, and for a not inconsiderable number of males the climax may be reached within . . . 10 or 20 seconds after coital entrance.

Sexual Behavior in the Human Male
ALFRED KINSEY

The problem of premature ejaculation is uniquely one which can be resolved effectively and permanently.

Human Sexual Inadequacy
MASTERS AND JOHNSON

IN THE 1970S, AMERICA TOOK THE PHRASE "MAKE LOVE, not war" to heart. We pulled out of Vietnam and embraced a new, open approach to sexual love. In our media, literature, arts and sciences, in schools, in public and private life, a sexual revolution was under way, touching everybody in one way or another.

In 1974, I was an undergraduate at the University of Michigan. I played varsity golf, served in the student government, wrote film reviews for the *Daily*, functioned as social chairman of the Sigma Chi fraternity, and ran amok with my sweetheart. In short, I did my all-American darndest to suck the marrow out of college life.

As a senior, I happened to take two classes that started me on a journey of more than fifteen years and eventually led to this book on mystical sex. The first was a general undergraduate course in human sexuality. The other, taught through the School of Education and entitled "Teaching Machines," was a course in self-directed, or programmed, learning.

In Human Sexuality we learned among other "facts" that the male sexual dysfunction called "premature ejaculation" was not only the most widespread of all sexual problems, but also the most easily remedied. (Kinsey after all said that three-fourths of all men reached a climax within two minutes after intromission. Masters and Johnson claimed a 98-percent cure rate.)

Teaching Machines was a course on how to construct a self-help booklet so that a given task could be learned without the need for a teacher and could be taught instead via pre-recorded self-instruction materials.

It wasn't long before a cloud formed over my head, filled with exclamation points and dollar signs. Of course! I would create a self-instruction program based on that 98-percent successful treatment for premature ejaculation and alleviate the suffering of three-fourths of the male population and their part-

2

ners. It would sell like hotcakes, I told myself. It would be so hot, it would have to be printed on asbestos. I'd skyrocket to fame: the Carson show . . . movie sale . . . Nobel Prize . . . ah, youth!

My adolescent delusions of grandeur were so compelling that I began a graduate study of psychology. This was, I reasoned, the logical way to gain the practical clinical experience needed to formulate, test, and refine my self-help book on premature ejaculation, and to give me the credentials to market it.

The early years of my doctoral curriculum were augmented through specialized professional training programs: at the Institute for Sex Research, founded by Alfred Kinsey at Indiana University; the Masters and Johnson Institute in St. Louis, which was then called the Reproductive Biology Research Foundation; the Center for Marital and Sexual Studies in Long Beach, California, directed by Bill Hartman and Marilyn Fithian, who were at that time known in professional circles as the Masters and Johnson of the West Coast; and at professional conferences sponsored by such organizations as the American Association of Sex Educators, Counselors and Therapists, and the Society for the Scientific Study of Sex. I also did volunteer work as a contraception counselor at the University of Michigan Student Health Service; directed and hosted my own radio show, "The Psychology of Sex," on the Campus Broadcast Network; helped formulate the original human sexuality sequence at the U of M Medical School, for which I lectured for many years; and served as a member of the university's multidisciplinary Council on Sexuality and Health Care. All in all, sexologically speaking, I was getting hip.

Those were the golden years for sexual therapy and research. Between 1970 and 1974, four substantial summaries and interpretations of the status of sexual behavior modification emerged: those by Masters and Johnson, Hartman and Fithian, Helen Singer Kaplan, and Jack Annon. Written and documented

3

by physicians and psychologists, these texts were enormously persuasive. Also in full swing were four journals devoted to the study of human sexuality, namely, the very scholarly *Archives of Sexual Behavior* and *Journal of Sex Research*, as well as the *Journal of Sex Education and Therapy* and *Medical Aspects of Human Sexuality*. It was easy to lose sight of the fact that the word "sexology" was a neologism, a new word, a new concept: medicine's authority in sexual matters.

Sexual therapy was enjoying its heyday largely because it was at the forefront of a full-scale war within the field of psychiatry, waged between the "modern" behavioral therapists and the "traditional" psychoanalysts. Behavior therapists pointed to the dramatic and impressive claims of Masters and Johnson and other sex therapists as proof that psychoanalysis was clumsy and outdated, like "building an elaborate garage to fix a flat tire." Behavioral sex therapy was given a great deal of visibility and credence by a large group of practitioners within the field of psychotherapy.

Since the 1920s, behaviorists had treated psychological problems as learned habits that could relatively quickly and directly be desensitized or reconditioned by patients' performing specific therapeutic relearning exercises. The procedure I was putting into the form of a self-help booklet and testing as part of my doctoral dissertation was precisely that—directions for a relearning-reconditioning behavior modification exercise through which men could learn to control their sexual excitement.

And what a bombastic booklet it would become. By 1978, after four years and four radically differing editions, there emerged, in its own words:

> . . . an appropriate potpourri of procedures for pro-
> longing the protuberance of your peduncle. It's a
> primary program that positively puts a plethora of
> precious procrastination-power into the poor old per-
> formance of yours.

The booklet was 135 pages of hysteria, in both the popular and, unfortunately, clinical senses. For men "vexed by the sex reflex hex" because of the immediate surroundings in which they made love, there were the "Five Environmental Protection Agencies for Emission Control." Even for the wife who could not motivate her rapidly responding husband to employ the treatment instructions ("Do you feel like the teller in a sperm bank?"), there was the "Three-Part Plan to Persuade Your Premature Partner to Participate in the Program." With regard to psychiatry's officious handling of sex, humorist James Thurber observed, "The heavy writers had got sex down and were breaking its arm." Clearly, I'd gone too far in the other direction.

Nevertheless, it had been with some confidence that in 1976, some colleagues and I opened an outpatient psychiatric care facility in suburban Detroit, with the intention of making it a clinical center for sex education, therapy, and research. Blue Cross/Blue Shield of Michigan paid us fifty dollars per forty-five minutes of behavioral treatment for any sexual dysfunction or "psychophysiologic genitourinary disorder"—each with its own diagnosis in the *International Classification of Diseases*. I began to publish articles in academic journals and textbooks and to deliver formal presentations at professional conferences throughout Europe and North America. In August 1976, I presented a paper entitled *Instructional Systems in the Modification of Male Sexual Behavior* to the International Symposium on Sex Education and Therapy in Stockholm. (The mayor of Stockholm honored the presenters with a luncheon at the City Hall, which is, coincidentally, where Nobel Prizes are awarded.)

I thought my systematic inquiry into the related psychological and sexological literature was providing the field with valuable new discoveries. I learned for example, that turn-of-the-century social reformers in America had widely prescribed the basic Masters and Johnson sex therapy technique for the treatment of premature ejaculation, but mainly as a birth-control

5

method and an acknowledgment of the existence of female sexual response, something not widely talked about at that time. Furthermore, I found that this same treatment procedure was also common to a curious body of ancient, so-called esoteric literature in China and India, which recommended prolonged lovemaking as a "mystical union" with the cosmos, and a method of achieving an altered state of consciousness.

I saw, in *The Tao of Sex* by Akira Ishihara and Howard Levy, an exact description of one of Master's and Johnson's techniques for treating premature ejaculation. This technique did not appear in their book, *Human Sexual Inadequacy*, but had been presented in St. Louis as part of their training program for professionals, which I'd attended in 1974.

What was the most advanced medical knowledge doing in second-century Chinese writings? At that time, I simply took it as confirmation that the modern sex therapy techniques had withstood the test of time. But more significantly, I had been introduced to an important segment of the world's religious literature.

It was something of an accident that even before entering college, I'd begun to learn about mystical psychology of the East and West, and the "worldly" religions and philosophies. Beginning in the 1960s and continuing for many years, one of Detroit's avant-garde FM radio stations would fulfill its "community service" minimum broadcast requirements by airing each Sunday morning the scholarly but profoundly amusing tapes of Alan Watts on philosophy, psychology, Zen, and comparative religion. These were fascinating to me, and I continued to study the history of religion as an undergraduate and beyond.

Inevitably, my interest in the worldly religions ran parallel to my study of human sexuality: on the one hand, I was looking deeper into the field of psychology from an academic perspective and gaining clinical experience in treating a wide variety of marital, sexual, and other personal and family problems. On the other, I was continuing to research many curious, arcane literary sources, East and West, and giving more thought to their deeper philosophical relevance in modern life. This two-fold path would reveal that psychologically, there are only two kinds of religion—mysticism and popular theology—and that they are based on the two kinds of thinking linked to the two hemispheres of the human brain.

The right brain hemisphere is involved with the physical and emotional feelings of the five senses and the sixth sense of intuition. The left hemisphere is associated with imagination and concepts, such as language and pictures seen in one's "mind's eye." Put simply, mysticism is religion based on right-brain, feeling consciousness; popular theology refers to left-brain, verbal religion.

This inner, organic difference between religions explains why mysticism promotes sensual experience of all kinds, while popular theology represses sensual feeling. Nowhere is this difference between religions more evident than in their opposing views on sex.

There is a large body of sophisticated twentieth-century literature on mystical religion, but it has largely gone unnoticed by the public, even by the so-called New Age movement, which claims to be involved in such matters. It is a very scholarly literature, but it is mistakenly dismissed out of hand as unscientific by most medical and psychological authorities.

Not that medicine's approach to sex is all that scientific. Looking back I realize that the professional literature and research have been riddled with deficiencies, shortcomings, oversights, and coverups. I discovered that even the clinical methods used by leading professionals were at times sophomoric, even slipshod. It became evident that there are actually relatively few men who report premature ejaculation to a professional as a presenting problem; that many, if not most, men who have problems controlling their climaxes do not have cooperative sexual partners, even if they're married; that many men who reverse their patterns of rapid ejaculation do not necessarily report an improved marriage. Furthermore, the actual behavioral techniques described in major texts and at training seminars are often seriously flawed. In fact, the clinical reporting of such cases has been significantly inadequate, with little or no physical, social, psychological, or marital data ever mentioned. There is not even an agreed-upon *definition* of premature ejaculation.

I also discovered that when the behavioral sex therapists claimed a 98-percent success rate, as Masters and Johnson had done in their *Human Sexual Inadequacy*, and when they stated that premature ejaculation is "virtually always amenable to the brief treatment procedures," as Helen Singer Kaplan had said in *The New Sex Therapy*, what they really meant was that treatment is virtually always successful *if* the man and woman follow the program. They neglected to mention that many men will *not* follow the therapeutic regime. More important, no one had sought to explain *why* so many men do not take advantage of such widely available information.

The reasons a couple would or would not follow the simple instructions involved their motivations, inhibitions, their emotional defenses, conscious or unconscious, as well as their intrapsychic and interpersonal issues. These were as complex and individual as each of the persons involved, and were related to their early experiences; bonding with parents; adolescent sexual imprinting; sexual experience at any age; learned attitudes— family, social, and cultural; education about sex, love, and male-female relationships; the meaning of sex and intimacy to an individual and a relationship; the way a couple communicates in general; a couple's physical and mental chemistry. Of course! After all, "The degree and kind of a man's sexuality reach up into the ultimate pinnacle of his spirit," as Nietzsche put it.

And so, by the time they were finished, my booklet, my

dissertation, and my Ph.D. were of sinking consolation. I'd become disillusioned with sexual therapy and research. I'd lost interest in saving the manhood of mankind and in skyrocketing to fame and fortune. It wasn't that sexual dysfunction suddenly seemed greasy, or self-help undignified. I finally had to admit to myself that medical science's psychiatric approach to sex (which Thomas Szasz aptly called *Sex by Prescription*) necessarily and profoundly missed the real meaning and issues of sex, or anyway the ones that interested me. Above all, I had come to realize that the spirituality of sex has nothing in particular to do with medicine or psychiatry, which view sex on a continuum between normal and pathodysfunctional.

But what, exactly, is meant by "spirituality," sexually or otherwise? For popular theology, the spiritual world is the imaginary, abstract, make-believe world, in which unicorns, fairies, Santa Clauses, witches, devils, and gods and goddesses seem to have a tangible reality of their own. It is the left brain hemisphere's world of conceptualization, which if thought to exist outside the imagination would be superstition. To encourage people to live within their imaginations, popular theology seeks to restrict sensual, right-hemisphere connections with the physical world. This is why popular theology consistently forbids sex.

The church fathers followed the lead of St. Augustine, who affirmed that "Nothing is so much to be shunned as sex relations." Celibacy, even within marriage, was the spiritual rule for all Christendom. The sex act was permitted only when intended to induce fertilization—even then, passion and physical sensation were taboo. A man should "inject the semen into the womb through the female genitalia as innocently as the menstrual flow is now ejected," St. Augustine told us in his *City of God*. John Calvin reminded Protestants that it was inexcusable for a wife to grasp that part of her husband's anatomy "from the sight and touch of which all chaste women naturally recoil."

The *Malleus Maleficarum*, used officially as a guidebook

for almost three hundred years by the church's Holy Inquisition to detect, torture, and kill witches, concluded that "All witchcraft comes from carnal lust, which in women is insatiable."

Sex repression is equally operant in Asian popular theology. Buddhism and Confucianism are exceedingly puritanical. In Hinduism, aside from the begetting of children, Swami Prabhupada tells us in his *Bhagavad-Gita As It Is*:

> One has to observe complete abstinence from sex life . . . One has to practice controlling the mind and avoiding all kinds of sense gratification, of which sex life is the chief.

For popular theology, spiritual sex is no sex at all. Sex is dealt with from an attitude of a paranoid hostility, which is only tolerated today because no one takes it seriously anymore. Abstinence as a form of sexual expression—it's kind of kinky if you think about it.

Why are the popular theologies so concerned about sex? Certainly, there is the political element of mass control—of reproduction, recreation, pleasure, values, and love. This is one reason sex was so prominent in the struggle within psychiatry. The collective control of people's sex lives can be a cultural nose ring by which large groups are led this way and that. If religion is the medicine of the world and the opiate of the masses, then sex is one of that drug's most active ingredients. Yet sex control is only one example, if a supreme one, of popular theology's attempt to move people's consciousness out of the sensual right brain hemisphere and into the conceptual left.

Today it is widely recognized that popular theology offers little practical insight into the spirituality of sex. Instead, our culture looks to *doctors* for some special kind of knowledge about sexuality. But what do doctors know about sex? Let me tell you.

Before 1970, there was very little, if any, instruction about sexuality in the medical schools. As recently as 1973, in a survey of University of Pennsylvania medical students, twenty-two percent of those questioned said that masturbation was a contributory factor in mental illness. Thankfully, within ten years virtually every medical school had a "Human Sexuality Sequence," an organized series of lectures and presentations that typically covered every sexual part, act, function, dysfunction, deviance, norm, and nuance. There could be a panel of homosexual advocates, data on historic and cross-cultural sexual customs, sexual behavior changes through the life cycle, and often a special, highly intensive, weekend-long "Sexual Attitude Reassessment." This SAR usually comprises intensive lectures and films—some call them therapeutic, some pornographic—which are interspersed with professionally facilitated small group meetings so medical students can express their feelings, ask questions, see the responses of others, and generally handle and accept it all.

I'm not against this kind of training for physicians, and I disagree with very little of the material presented. I think the programs are actually quite good. It's just that they must be recognized for what they are: the indoctrination of young doctors with the current vogue of psychiatric sexual dogma, including its proclaimed authority over our sexual feelings and behavior—which no one seems to question—and its emphasis on sex as compared with other areas of human life.

For example, in medical school there are, of course, lectures on how the digestive system functions, but there is little or no instruction on the norms or deviations of eating behavior, historic or cross-cultural eating trends and taboos, or statistics on the various styles of cooking. There is no panel to discuss deviant table manners, no intensive weekend to adjust one's attitudes toward the different tastes of food, issues of nutrition, or the politics of starving countries, or the advertising and sale of food products, or eating disorders.

Despite all that doctors are taught about sex, they have no

training in the transpersonal function of sex whatsoever. They are almost uniquely unqualified to speak about that aspect of sex which is the most important, most essential aspect of sexuality—the one that reaches to the "ultimate pinnacle of the human experience." Nor is the spirituality of sex discussed in the otherwise very well done professional texts and training programs, journals, and conferences.

Medicine doesn't *forbid* sex, but does attempt to *control* it. Psychiatric sex dogma confines sexual behavior to a strict set of parameters. Psychiatry doesn't openly ridicule or prohibit sex. In fact, it may seem to permit and even encourage sex. It goes further—it *insists* on sex. If you don't want sex, you are psychiatrically diagnosed as having a "disorder of sexual desire" (Kaplan published a book by that title). Women who have trouble reaching climax are psychiatrically labeled for their *syndrome* (anorgasmia) as surely and coldly as unmarried women who easily have orgasms are labeled by the church for their *sin*. The *Diagnostic and Statistical Manual* of the American Psychiatric Association has stated that man is a premature ejaculator if he does not have "voluntary control over the ejaculatory reflex." He is branded with a mental-disorder code number from the *International Classification of Diseases* despite the fact that a reflex is an action, which by definition must occur involuntarily.

Sixteen centuries earlier, St. Augustine declared that "The sexual members, like all the rest, should be moved by the command of the will. . . . As would be proper, a voluntary control would employ them." "Voluntary" meaning according to approved guidelines.

But pleasure is okay now. It's good. Sex is good for you. It's *healthy*. Like sleep or nutrition. One of today's medical treatments for male sexual dysfunction was mocked by Dr. Szasz as "penile jogging."

Psychiatry's approach goes way beyond ancient matrimonialism that required sex for the procreation of children; it *insists* on sexual desire and pleasure. If you're not performing according to the whens, the hows, the whys and wherefores, the ifs and the buts that the American Psychiatric Association prescribes, you are by definition "sick." But don't worry, you can have your "treatment" covered by your health insurance company. From reaching a climax too quickly, to reaching a climax too slowly, to a lack of sexual feeling or desire—the parameters, right down to minute details—are all covered in the APA liturgy and form a range of acceptable, adequate—that is, literally and legally, *sane*—sexual conduct. Both man and wife *must* feel sexual interest and desire, become sexually aroused, and reach a climax, not too fast, but don't take too long, either! Fail to comply, and you will be urged to confess your disorderly conduct to a psychiatrist, psychologist, or other sex policeman who "should," we are told by the "experts" on sex therapy "ethics," be licensed by the appropriate governmental department. Then, if you are lucky, you will receive the secret "treatment" instructions to the sex exorcism through which you can enter the kingdom of psychiatric normality.

Promoting healthy sex, while it may be "good for you," makes sex a political matter over which medicine seeks to rule.

One wonders how doctors, psychologists, and other health professionals became involved with sexual behavior in the first place. For one thing, sex is at the center of one of psychiatry's most embarrassing secrets: that by 1900 the two major medical treatments of emotional disorders were animal magnetism (hypnosis) and electrotherapy, which routinely included the electrical stimulation of the genitals, regardless of the nature of the complaint.

This was not an obscure quack remedy. It was the standard accepted medical treatment of choice. Freud began his practice as a nerve magnetist and venereal electrocutioner, as Dr. Szasz has chronicled in his important *Myth of Psychotherapy*. Nor is this ancient history: as late as 1948, in their mainstream medical textbook, *Sexual Disorders in the Male*, Drs. Walker and Strauss recommended their special chair for the electric stimulation of the testicles.

Freud would later acknowledge that electrotherapy was a deliberately fake "placebo" treatment, "my pretense treatment," a make-believe, "magic" treatment that allowed him to "keep in touch" with his patients. Although he would abandon electrotherapy in favor of talk therapy, Freud would maintain that the neuroses, without exception, were disturbances of sexual functioning.

Electrotherapy has gone out of vogue. Hooray. But it was replaced by pharmaceutical chemotherapy, the standard psychiatric fare of today, which in many ways is equally bogus and bizarre. In the case of the psychiatric "illness" called premature ejaculation, drugs including sedatives, tranquilizers, antidepressants, female hormones, appetite suppressants, and topical anesthetics have all been recommended in the published professional literature by leading, well-meaning, postwar physician-sexologists. Even as late as 1949, one *Journal of Urology* article endorsed the application of cocaine to the glans penis prior to intercourse.

It sounds funny now, but in 1976 in a semiserious effort to replicate the topical anesthetic treatment studies cited in leading professional journals, I availed myself of a tube of Ultra-Staylong (three-percent benzocaine), one of countless mail-order ointments, creams, and sprays with names such as Sta-Hard, Longtime Mannercreme, Linger, Detaine, and Mr. Prolong. (Such anesthetic chemicals as benzocaine and novocaine are primarily used in surgery to paralyze perceptual sensation from the region to which they are applied so that, from a tactile point of view, the affected part of the anatomy . . . disappears! To say the least, it was not funny at the time, sexwise; and of course, the studies were not replicated.) With a clarity momentarily bordering on the surreal, I had experienced firsthand medicine's superstrange, and above all perversely antispiritual, attitude toward sex. An attitude designed to bring sexual love under the control of medicine at all costs, in this case by "treating" it with drugs.

Perhaps the weirdest medicated goof of all began in the early 1960s when the powerful antipsychotic drug, thioridizine, notably prescribed in the treatment of schizophrenia under the brand names Thorazine and Mellaril, was recommended in the medical literature and prescribed by doctors in the treatment of rapid ejaculation. The reason was that one of its gross side effects is "dry" and presumably retrograde ejaculation, wherein the man's semen flows into his bladder rather than being normally, visibly ejaculated. It was not until 1976 that it was shown in a singularly honest study by Dr. J. Kotin and his colleagues, who actually tried the drug themselves, that not only does thioridizine *not* delay orgasm or prolong intercourse, but it actually causes severe sexual dysfunction in men, especially impotence and painful orgasms.

Today the approved medical treatment of premature ejaculation does not include usage of these drugs. But their wide and continuous prescription attested to psychiatry's historic attempt to make sexual lovemaking into a medical endeavor.

That neither popular theology nor medicine offers a meaningful, higher understanding of sex is one reason that so many of our society's internal controversies and problems have to do with sex: pornography, sexual harassment, child molestation, spouse abuse, rape, abortion, contraception, sex education, AIDS and other sexually transmitted diseases, homosexuality, extramarital sex, premarital sex, and unwed teenage motherhood.

The same era that saw medicine's effort to bring sex into the open also witnessed the deaths of many of the world's most prominent thinkers on the subject of mysticism—Alan Watts and Julius Evola, for example, and more recently Mircea Eliade and Joseph Campbell—whose voices we will hear in the coming chapters. These writers had penetrated the intrapersonal and transpersonal aspects of sex by examining, translating, and interpreting the history of the mystical traditions.

What, then, is spirituality from a mystical perspective? For mysticism, the spiritual world is the physical cosmos, the real world of energy and matter that we can perceive directly through our senses and intuition in right-brain consciousness. Mysticism encourages our physical connection with the cosmos, our sensual involvement with and experience of the natural world, a unity with the environment, with what is "not me." The sexual unity of lovers is mysticism's favorite example of true oneness with the universe. For the same reason that popular theology forbids sex, mysticism encourages it.

The mystical literature details a special approach to lovemaking which maximizes intimacy and spontaneous creativity—an approach to sex beyond procreation and mere pleasure, one that brings about a high feeling, an altered state of mind, or "mystical experience." To demonstrate this single vision of sexuality common to all the mystical traditions, this book will define and explain mysticism, discuss mysticism's approach to sexual lovemaking, and apply mysticism and mystical sex to a monogamous love relationship.

So come with me now on a holy and enchanted journey. We will travel across the peaks of civilization itself, with its cycles of genius, conversion, and conquest. We'll explore forces that at times unified North and South, East and West, and at times destroyed whole cultures, burning them, plowing them under, covering them with salt. Our journey will span centuries, millennia of history, from the earliest matriarchies, to the courts and temples of ancient China and India, to the castles of semi-Christian medieval Europe, and venture ahead to consider the meaning of sex in the year 2000. We will go past sexuality and into the realms of science, religion, politics, and language, linked together by the concept and practice of mystical sex.

1

Mysticism, Mystical Experience, and Mystical Sex

There are, indeed, things that cannot be put into words. They make themselves manifest/they show themselves. They are what is mystical.

Tractatus Logico-Philosophicus
LUDWIG WITTGENSTEIN

The great periods of art and culture are always connected with an erotic-mystical revival.

Shiva and Dionysus
ALAIN DANIÉLOU

I DO NOT NOW, NOR HAVE I EVER, SPORTED A TALL, CONE-shaped hat, embroidered with planets and signs of the zodiac. Nor is the term mysticism, as I use it, associated with the supernatural, magic, make-believe, or anything unrealistic, high-falutin, or phony. Nor do I apply the adjective mystical to that which is simply mysterious or mystifying, as it is sometimes loosely used in common speech.

Because so much is misunderstood about mysticism, it is the purpose of this chapter to carefully define and briefly describe mysticism, its philosophy, its long history, and its use of sexual love to promote an altered state of consciousness or "mystical experience." We will consider the theory of the two brain hemispheres and their "modes" of thinking, ways of thinking that correspond in turn to the two types of religion—mysticism and popular theology—each with its characteristic attitudes about nature, society, and the individual. We will also explore mystical experience and how it can be achieved by means of mysticism's approach to sex, an approach emphasizing timelessness, spontaneity, and a meditative state of mind.

Although mysticism and mystical sex are intriguing, to say the least, it is not my intention to proselytize, to persuade, or to push mysticism as a better form of religion, or mystical sex as the right way to make love. I do, however, want to show it to be a real possibility that one can see through and beyond ideas, and that through sexual love one can experience and appreciate that which cannot be described: the mystical.

Two Kinds of Thinking, Two Kinds of Religion

Modern medical and scientific knowledge about the brain and the mechanism of thinking is extremely sparse. We really don't know very much about it at all. From studying the effects of head and brain injuries and through other physiological and psychological experimentation, there has emerged in recent decades a theory about two different modes of thinking, styles of thought attributed to the left and right hemispheres of the brain.

According to this theory, the right side of the brain (which controls the left hand and, in general, the left side of the body) is most often associated with the direct sensual experience of the five sense organs and the "sixth sense" of intuitive thinking—that is, "feelings" of some kind, feelings that can be a result of a person's interaction with the external environment, as in direct sense perception or spontaneous creativity. Or they can be a reaction to one's own internal states (proprioception), which are often involved with emotional feelings and so-called altered states of consciousness.

On the other hand—the right hand—the left hemisphere of the brain is generally associated with the process of conceptualization in its many forms, including the powers of symbolic imagination and those functions related to language: labeling, categorizing, verbal rule following (logic), and rule following in general. The left hemisphere mode has been likened to a computer screen, on which the whole gamut of concepts and computations can be portrayed and manipulated in the "mind's eye."

These two styles of thinking also serve as the two ends of a spectrum, according to which we can view the world's major historic and cross-cultural religious movements. Those religions featuring an emphasis on the sensual, right hemisphere mode of thought are the mystical traditions; those emphasizing the abstract, imaginative left mode are the popular theologies.

Some examples of popular theology are Confucianism in China; Hinduism and later Buddhism in India; and in the Western world, Greco-Roman religion and later Judeo-Christianity and Islam. Mystical traditions include Taoism in China; Tantrism in India; and in the Mediterranean world, the mysteries and, later, Gnosticism—which evolved to become Alchemy, Kabbalism, and Chivalry.

The fact that religiocultural movements organically reflect the two kinds of human consciousness explains many of the historically recurrent similarities and differences among the world's religions. It explains why, for example, the sense-oriented mystical traditions tend to encourage physical pleasure and gala experience, including sexual lovemaking, while the concept-bound popular theologies forbid such sensual experience in favor of the imagination of, or belief in, certain stories and symbols.

Mysticism identifies spirituality with the physical cosmos, and urges people to experience sensually their physical unity with the natural environment. Sex is recommended by the mystical religions because it is a most natural way to feel one's actual connection with the cosmos, with what is "not me."

At the same time, this physical unity between the person and his or her outside world is precisely why all popular theologies (such as Christianity) are so obsessively paranoid about sex. And not only sex, but the celebration of sensual experience and altered states of consciousness of *all* kinds, whether they are brought about by dancing, alcohol, music, or any other creative or direct sensory feeling.

Conversely, popular theology equates spirituality with various conceptual constructs—images, symbols, and words—and urges its followers to picture those images so clearly, so realistically, that they believe their conceptualizations actually exist outside their imaginations. This is why the central issue in Christianity (to use a familiar example) is whether or not one "believes in Jesus Christ," that is, believes in the literal truth of the church's conception of Jesus Christ: that he was the Son of God, that he died for the remission of sins, and so on.

Each popular theology has its own plot and characters that

it wants people to believe in. But the various symbols themselves are less relevant than the common act of conceptualizing, of imagining, of making believe, which is central to both popular theology and the left hemisphere mode of thought.

The difference between left and right hemisphere modes of thinking also explains why the world's popular theologies assign religious authority to special, permanent scriptures and words, and to an organized social class of clergymen/priests to administer those words, while the mystical traditions have no sacred texts or priesthood whatsoever. Instead they give religious authority to each individual on the basis of personal observation and intuition. The emphasis on personal observation is why, contrary to what most people realize, all major scientific progress has been associated with mysticism. What we call modern science was derived directly from the alchemists of the European Renaissance, such as Newton and Paracelsus, who, in turn, inherited the historic attitude of empirical scientific inquiry from the earlier mystical traditions.

In his *Forge and the Crucible*, the Romanian-born historian of religion, Mircea Eliade traced the evolution of Alchemy from prehistoric metallurgy to modern chemistry; it was always carried along within the mystical traditions of each culture.

> Everywhere we find alchemy, it is always intimately related to a "mystical" tradition: in China with Taoism, in India with Yoga and Tantrism, in Hellenicism in Egypt with gnosis, in Islamic countries with hermetic and esoteric mystical schools, in the Western Middle Ages and Renaissance with Hermeticism, Christian and sectarian mysticism, and Cabala.

Not only scientific progress but creativity of all kinds is a historic function of mysticism. As Alain Daniélou, the foremost living interpreter of Indian religion, pointed out in his elucidating *Shiva and Dionysus*, "The great periods of art and culture are always connected with an erotic-mystical revival." This is not coincidence; creativity of all sorts is a function of the sensuality of the right hemisphere mode of thinking.

It is not surprising, then, to realize that popular theology often has fanatically opposed scientific progress and discovery, favoring instead the incessant ritual repetition of established ceremonies and reference to fixed verbal scriptures. The Christian church imprisoned and executed scientists such as Galileo for expressing the audacious idea that the earth was not flat, because the opening lines of the Bible are largely based on a stationary, flat-earth geography. For all popular theology, the Word, the Book—whether the Bible, the Koran, or the Analects—is given more credence and authority than the natural cosmos itself.

Of course, theories, myths, fables, fairy tales, and other conceptualizations such as numbers, time, and musical notation can be very useful in their place, for instruction and entertainment. But they become superstitious when taken to have actually transpired or to have a tangible existence of their own. As Joseph Campbell explained in his *Power of the Myth*:

> They were saying it is *as if* it were thus. The notion
> that someone literally made the world—that is what
> is known as artificialism. It is the child's way of
> thinking: The table is made, so somebody made the
> table. The world is here, so somebody must have
> made it.

Table 1 lists some of the differences between the left and right hemisphere modes of consciousness, which at the same time imply the differences between popular theology and mysticism.

Table 1

Modes of Consciousness

Left Hemisphere Mode of Consciousness	Right Hemisphere Mode of Consciousness
Conceptualizing	Sensing/perceiving
Theoretical imagination	Physical connection
Thinking	Feeling
Logic	Intuition
Ritual	Creativity
Role play	Spontaneity
Morality	Compassion
Dogma	Empiricism: direct observation of nature
Supernatural	Natural
Superstition	Science
Repetition/fixation	Evolution
Technology	Ecology
Asceticism: sense deprivation	Celebration
Monarchy/totalitarianism	Democracy
Popular theology	Mysticism

This formulation of religious types represents the two extreme ends of a broad spectrum of possibilities, but it does clarify the essential, organic contrast between the two types of religion. In practice, except during periods of extreme social severity, a given culture will have both kinds of religions operating simultaneously, at times in peace and at times in violent opposition, in much the same way that a person's two modes of thinking can operate intrapsychically, sometimes in a coordinated harmony, sometimes in a dysphoric imbalance—an imbalance that may be at the root of many so-called mental disorders.

The many ways in which the two sorts of thinking are manifested by the two types of religion may be illustrated if we look at the larger cultural movements that contained them. Let us, then, paint with very broad strokes the historical contexts in which some of the various mystical traditions appeared. We will see how mankind's first civilizations were mystical, that is, based on a right hemisphere orientation; how they were crushed by our patriarchal forefathers, whose social organization was left hemisphere dominated; and how mysticism would reblossom during the eras of major cultural advance.

Early History of Mysticism

Even as recently as the turn of this century, it was still widely debated whether God had created the earth, man, and everything else in 4963 B.C. as some theologians argued, or in 4004 B.C. as other scholars recommended. Despite its obvious invalidity, the relevance of this debate had not been successfully challenged until Darwin's time, little more than a hundred years ago.

In reality, by 5000 B.C., human civilization had been flourishing for many, many centuries—since long, long before Jesus and the Romans, long before Plato, Buddha, and Confucius, before Homer and Moses, before Abraham. Twenty-five hundred years before Jesus Christ lived and died, that is, forty-five centuries ago, a culture of loosely connected nations reached from China and India to the Atlantic Ocean. Over the previous two millennia, these societies had made advancements in agriculture, metallurgy, astronomy, and mathematics, which would not be surpassed until relatively modern history.

Connected by water travel for a thousand years, these nations were centered either on large islands, such as Britain, Malta, and Crete, or where major rivers entered oceans, as where the Indus flows into the Indian Ocean, the Tigris and Euphrates into the Persian Gulf, and the Nile into the Mediterranean.

The nations of this cultural era were not exactly alike, but they shared many features. Animal husbandry and agriculture were advanced. Intricate spoken language, ideographic writing, and number systems had long been used in China, Egypt, and the British Isles to express complex generalized principles. Sophisticated, and in some ways refined, smelting, casting, and other metalworking techniques were prevalent and knowledgeably used with copper, silver, gold, tin, lead, zinc, carbon, sulphur, mercury, and later iron.

Giant stone or megalith sculptures appeared in every part of mankind's first culture, from the Atlantic to the Indian oceans, evolving into huge theaters, pyramids, henges (circles), and other geometrically and astronomically arranged configurations. Stonehenge and the Pyramids are singularly famous remnants of this culture, but they are by no means alone or rare. There remain twelve hundred megaliths from this period in the British Isles alone.

These giant stone time capsules stand as incontrovertible evidence that forces us to recognize an incredibly advanced civilization. Their mathematical, astronomical, and philosophical themes could not be fully deciphered until modern times,

25

because our civilization had not attained their level of sophistication. The testimony of the megaliths may still not be entirely understood, and it is certainly not appreciated.

These evolving cultures shared one religion, which would serve as the prototype for all mystical traditions that followed. This religion did not "worship" God, or anything else, as we think of worship. It involved a love for nature and the study of the ways or principles of nature, which were personified and often referred to as Bacchus. Bacchus represented the unity of nature—above and below, man and woman, Hermes and Aphrodite. From India to the Atlantic, each country had its own name for a similar system of natural principles: Shiva in India, Osiris in Egypt, Dionysus on Crete, Bacchus in Greece, and in China, the depersonalized Tao. But these were variations in name only. The religions of these countries tended to share a common symbolism, theory, and attitude of life. Concluded Daniélou, "There is no difference in concept or practice between the Shivaite Bakhtas or Dionysiac Bacchants."

The overall bacchic approach to culture can be summarized according to several themes, three of which we will call celebration, chivalry, and creativity in the arts and sciences. These three principles would be reflected in the mystical movements whenever they were revived throughout history. Let us touch on these three principles in order to better understand mankind's first great culture and the later mystical traditions based on its civilization. If we seem to focus on Eurasian traditions, it is because we have found more of their artifacts, buildings, and written documents. Other regions of the world may well have had comparable cultures.

Celebration

Popular wisdom identifies Bacchus as the god of wine and drunkenness, which is true. But that personification is only a small part of a much greater interest and emphasis on altered states of consciousness of all sorts. The celebrants of Bacchus—bacchoi in Greece, bhaktas in India—achieved elevated states of gala consciousness by many means: for example, by music, singing, and dancing, sometimes in a carnival procession to the hills, to eat, drink, be merry, and pursue happiness. The bacchic celebrants danced as young people do today, in groups, with no one particular partner—dancing all together to the rhythmic beating music and singing, exuberant dancing to feel that high experience that comes from absorption and spontaneity. As Euripides wrote in his play *The Bacchae*, "Whirling feet kept time to the strict beat of the taut hide and the squeal of the wailing flute."

In addition to wine, dance, music, and song, the bacchanalian celebration could take the form of love and mystical sex exactly as it is presented in this book. The whole notion of mystical sex evolved from bacchic celebration, that is, sex not for procreation or mere pleasure, but instead as a transcendental unity with one's lover and a subsequent altered state of consciousness.

Historians have often wrongly interpreted the many forms of bacchanalian celebration, such as group dancing and mystical sex, to be fertility rites, superstitious and deluded rituals performed to elicit magic reproductive favoritism from nature. But, to quote from Eliade's *History of Religious Beliefs and Ideas:*

> Aphrodite will never become the goddess of fertility
> *par excellence.* It is physical love, carnal union which
> she inspires, exalts and defends. . . . Under the disguise of a frivolous divinity is hidden one of the deepest sources of religious experience: the revelation of
> sexuality as transcendence and mystery.

Furthermore, the attempt to gain personal advantage, success, or protection with regard to fertilization, the weather, or anything else by means of rites, ritual, casting spells, prayer, sacrifices, and other bilateral transactions with supernatural beings, is a characteristic of popular theology, and is categorically alien to mysticism.

The purpose of bacchanalian events was to experience an altered state of consciousness, the celebration of nature by physical unity with nature. In this sensual, physical unity with the cosmos, we see reflected an emphasis on the right-brain hemisphere mode of mental activity. This is also one way of understanding the principle of mystical unity or oneness with the universe. Bacchic celebration provided a direct physical experience of the world via sense perception, as distinct from imagining the world according to supposedly authoritative measurement and description.

Chivalry

The second theme that Bacchus represented was the political, religious, and legal equality of men and women, a theme I will call chivalry.

We are all somewhat familiar with the notion of romantic love and the social movement of the European Middle Ages called Chivalry, which was part of the reflowering of mystical principles that led to the Renaissance. In romantic literature and poetry to this day, chivalry represents the protection, love, and even worship of women within the context of a patriarchal society. But the original chivalry was more fundamental. It was the recognition of the inseparability, the mutual, equal need of men and women for each other. "Dionysus is a democratic god," concluded Dodds in *Euripides' Bacchae*.

In bacchic culture, the mutual need and inseparability of the sexes was exemplified by the principles of androgyny and the hermaphrodite. Androgyny is the idea that everyone, every woman and every man, has both a male and a female aspect in his or her character. The hermaphrodite symbolizes the notion that each man or woman is merely half a human being, who becomes fully human only when paired with a partner. The hermaphrodite, then, is the macrocosmic symbol of male-female unity, of which the individual is a part, while androgyny is the microcosmic perspective of the unity occurring within each individual. One goal of bacchic culture, and of future mystical traditions, was harmony, balance, and unity between men and women and between the male and female aspects within each person.

The divinity in bacchic culture, accordingly, was not a solely female or male figure, but on earth both male (andro) and female (gyne), and in heaven both Hermes and Aphrodite; hence our words androgyny and hermaphrodite. The fact that women were put on an equal footing with men made these cultures appear relatively female dominated to the patriarchal tribes who would conquer them, and hence they have been historically referred to as matriarchies. However, they were not societies in which women ruled men, but rather cultures in which men and women were in harmony in another manifestation of the theme of mystical unity.

Of course, androgyny and the hermaphrodite are, as we all know, psychological conditions. They exist above and beyond the biochemical facts that as adults we each have male and female hormones within us; that from the moment of conception, half of our genetic material comes from each sex; or the anatomical-physiological existence of men's nipples and women's clitorises.

However, as with many matriarchal mystical symbols, the androgyne and the hermaphrodite often degenerated into meaningless and self-serving figments of random imagination, and were attached to practices that had nothing in particular to do with mysticism. This distortion is explored in Eliade's *Mephistopheles and the Androgyne*:

The androgyne is understood by decadent writers simply as a hermaphrodite in whom both sexes exist anatomically and physiologically. They are concerned not with a wholeness resulting from the fusion of the sexes but with a superabundance of erotic possibilities. Their subject is not the appearance of a new type of humanity in which the fusion of the sexes produces a new unpolarized consciousness, but a self-styled sensual perfection, resulting from the active presence of both sexes in one. . . .

The decadent writers did not know that the hermaphrodite represented in antiquity an ideal condition which men endeavoured to achieve spiritually by means of imitative rites; but that if a child showed at birth any signs of hermaphroditism, it was killed by its own parents. In other words, the actual, anatomical hermaphrodite was considered an aberration of Nature or a sign of the gods' anger and consequently destroyed out of hand. Only the ritual androgyne provided a model, because it implied not an augmentation of anatomical organs but, symbolically, the union of the magico-religious powers belonging to both sexes.

It may not be difficult to accept the concept that we all have both male and female aspects. Yet when we try to say what exactly those masculine and feminine principles are, we find them exceedingly difficult to define. As we try to define them, we see that they have little or nothing to do with biology, sex, or even men or women.

The mystical literature and popular wisdom tell us that the feminine principle corresponds to the intuitive, creative, intimate, immediate, unitive, nourishing, sensuous, spontaneous aspects of our personalities. The masculine principle reflects the logical, labeling, theoretical, legalistic, boundary-conscious, rule-following, mission-oriented, competitive approach we are all capable of. In this categorizing of human traits, we recognize that we may not be referring to biophysical maleness or femaleness so much as to the left and right modes of psychological functioning within each of us, men and women alike.

Creativity

The final element of matriarchal culture that we will examine here is scientific and artistic creativity, a theme reflected in all later mystical revivals.

It is from bacchic culture that science as we think of it evolved. The direct, sensual perception of how things are, unclouded by preconceptions, is precisely what is meant by empiricism and scientific objectivity. This interest in science was not implied, sentimental, or vague, but overtly demonstrated. Ancient Egyptian treatises, for example, often had three levels or registers of discourse: the archetypal or theoretical ideal, the typal or real-life specific example, and the ectypal, the scientific principle behind both. We know beyond any possible doubt, simply by studying the arrangement of certain megaliths, that matriarchal culture developed sophisticated mathematics, geometry, and astronomy. Certain megaliths are aligned astronomically and according to triangular, circular, and other geometric shapes, in many cases using standard measures of length. Large and small stone objects were shaped into the major platonic solids or proportioned according to the Pythagorean theorem at least ten centuries before Plato or Pythagoras lived. Matriarchal inscription and architecture also employed the ratios π (pi), the key to figuring the circumference and area of a circle, and ϕ (phi), geometry's "golden proportion."

Numbers appear to us to be the language by which we reduce, decipher, translate, and understand nature. In describing his "geometry of thinking," Buckminster Fuller pointed out how nature invariably appears to us to do all its associating and dissociating by means of whole, rational numbers.

It is little wonder then that later mystical traditions shared a numerical myth about the origin of the universe: the division of the whole cosmos into two parts. Specifically, according to this symbolism, the infinite whole cosmos contracts, leaving a void, zero, and by comparison, everything else, one. Drawing on the work of Egyptologist Schwaller de Lubicz, two fascinating, concise, hands-on books, Robert Lawlor's *Sacred Geometry* and Andre Vandenbroeck's *Philosophical Geometry*, tell about sacred geometry's division of unity into two, a contraction allowing for "divine self-apperception." In his history of mathematics, *Number: The Language of Science*, Tobias Dantzig described how, by following this traditional mystical formula, Gottfried Leibniz around 1700 developed binary arithmetic, the base-2 number system of today's computers, which represents all numbers using only the digits 0 and 1.

Let us step back now, and ask whether this numerical beginning of the cosmos, this division of the whole into two parts, is not what the mind does to organize itself when it divides into left and right modes of thought. After all, there are no anatomical differences between the two brain hemispheres; and we are not born with two modes of thinking. The mystical myth of the numerical origin of the world is similar to what child psychologists tell us occurs in human mental development: We all, as infants, begin life in total right-mode sensuality, so that even the external world is perceived as an infinite extension of the self. As the infant's consciousness develops, what is really developing is the left-mode ability to form mental boundaries, primarily at first between self and other. Just as an eye cannot directly see itself, and an ear cannot hear itself, the right mode of consciousness cannot directly experience itself. But it can see the reflection of itself—a conceptual, cognitive-verbal representation in the mirror of theoretical imagination, or the "computer screen" of the left hemisphere mode of thinking. Unfortunately, many people begin to mistake themselves for their conceptual reflection of themselves; one of the goals of mysticism is to bring one's conceptualization into perspective and regain the original perceptual unity between oneself and the outside world.

Above all, science is an attitude toward life and the cosmos, not a fixed body of knowledge. It is an ever-renewed evolution, process of growth, and discovery of nature, which itself is always changing and evolving, impermanent and thereby indefinable.

In matriarchal culture, art and the concept of beauty were closely related to science and natural principles. Fine art and architecture, for example, were often based on mathematical and geometric proportions. The numerical structure of music was thought of as a connection between art and science, because one can directly and without thought or effort perceive sensually the mathematical principles inherent in harmonic progressions and combinations. The mathematics involved in a harmonic progression can be directly perceived aurally as harmony itself, without the listener's knowing anything about the mathematical aspects of octaves, sound waves, or vibratory frequency. At the same time, the actual sound is something that no amount of language can convey or describe. It can only be sensually perceived. Therefore, both the spontaneous act of creating and playing music and the sensation of hearing it are associated with the right hemisphere mode of consciousness. In sexual lovemaking as well, one can adopt a simultaneously creative, spontaneous approach, as we will see.

Finally, the spontaneous, artistic creating and experiencing of music, dance, or lovemaking brings us full circle, back to the gala exuberance of bacchanalian celebration. These three aspects of matriarchal culture—celebration, chivalry, and creativity—all have a great deal in common, not by coincidence, but because they are all organically associated with the sensual, creative, right brain hemisphere mode in both men and women.

Again, the matriarchal nations were not homogeneous. Some societies were more creative in the arts, others in science, others celebrated more, others sailed more, others built more, others were more chivalrous, others less. Furthermore, not every ancient example of art or science, sailing or metallurgy, or celebration was from the matriarchal era. But the fact that advanced human societies flourished simultaneously and maintained communication over many centuries allows us to speak of these different nations as a continuous culture, one which exhibited the characteristics that would be reflected in future mystical traditions.

But what happened to matrio-mystical culture? Let us look at the patriarchal tribes that crushed it and see how they built a civilization whose language, religion, social structure, and attitude toward life would form the basis of our civilization today and would provide the cultural background through which mysticism would blossom when it flowered in later historic eras.

The Fall of Civilization

Matriarchal culture flourished at its most dazzling in the ten centuries between, roughly, 2800 and 1800 B.C. Toward the latter half of this era, various towns, cities, and regions had begun to fall to invasions by two groups: Indo-Europeans from the north, and Semites from the south and east.

The Indo-European invaders included the Hittites, Indo-Iranians, Greeks, Romans, Celts, and many lesser known tribes. They lived a nomadic, land-traveling existence with a common sort of patriarchal religion and a stratified social structure, and they spoke from the common Indo-European family of languages.

The Semitic tribes, from the east and south, included the Assyrians, Babylonians, Phoenicians, Hebrews, Aramaeans, and others. They spoke from a common Afro-Asiatic family of languages, and were also organized as nomadic, patriarchal tribes. They would leave us such documents as Hammurabi's code and the Bible.

The glorification of the Indo-European invasions southward was a primary purpose of the epics attributed to "Homer," the name given to the collective historic writings of the early Greeks, compiled over roughly two hundred years. For the Indo-Europeans who conquered India, the epic *Mahabharata*, which is four times the length of the collected works of Homer, serves largely the same function: the glorification of their conquests as they invaded from the north.

Incidentally, it was about this time that "history," as it is popularly portrayed, began. The earlier, more sophisticated matriarchal cultures were, from that point onward, relegated to an aside, footnote, or allusion; they became minor and even mythical players on the social and religious scene of their conquerors.

These nomadic tribes settled in the formerly civilized regions and set about ruling the indigenous populations and their own in their new sedentary form of life. They quickly seized, assimilated, and further developed as much as they could from the matriarchal cultures, especially with respect to technological knowledge, as with their improvements of writing and metallurgy.

The patriarchal tribes were not necessarily evil or primitive, but their style of society featured three characteristics that stood in dramatic opposition to bacchic and later mystical tradition. Specifically, in contrast to the matriarchal emphasis on celebration, chivalry, and creativity in science and art, the patriarchies would favor sense deprivation or asceticism, an institutional class structure and subjugation of women, and the use of religious superstition for governmental and imperial purposes.

First, the nomadic patriarchies favored an ascetic, agonistic approach to life. That is, they renounced and denounced sensual feeling, pleasure, and especially altered consciousness; consequently, they would historically tend to forbid, in one extreme or another, drugs and drinking; dancing, singing, and music; and, in particular, sex—except as a specialized act for procreation.

When the patriarchal tribes encountered what we have described as bacchanalian celebration, they were shocked and horrified, and they wrote of it, as we still read in our histories, as frenzied, manic, libidinous, orgiastic, ecstatic, and dangerously, insanely enthusiastic. Some of the oldest writing of the Indo-Europeans who conquered bacchic India prays that India won't follow Shiva and the "phallus-worshipers," who were called "lascivious wretches" and "drug addicts." And, confusing altered states of gala celebration with insanity, Homer referred to Dionysus as a "madman, rejected by well-doers."

Imperial Rome is often thought of as having been sensually decadent. But Roman society was originally quite prudish, and only degenerated in its waning period. Even then, its greatest writers and satirists lamented Rome's moral decay. Furthermore, the grotesque and perverted sexual experiments of the Roman baths had nothing in particular to do with mystical sex, but were merely outrageous genital exercises in venereal titillation.

Second, in patriarchal society, women were officially held in servitude. Although they could be tended benignly or even lovingly, they were actually owned by men. (This condition was one of the first rules established in Genesis.) Legally, a woman was chattel, movable property sold by a father and bought by a husband, who then held the power of life and death over his wife and their children until his daughters were sold to other men. Such was the essence of the sales agreement known as the marriage contract. Dowries sometimes accompanied women in marriage because, in contrast to matriarchal culture, women could not inherit or otherwise own property in their own lifetimes.

With time, the subjugation of women was further manifested in many ways. At one extreme, the rape of undefended women in war and often in peacetime was expected and almost taken for granted. On another level, in a more gradual process, women were weaned from religious and political institutions, forbidden from the priesthood, and in some cases barred completely from the temples, where the goddesses were also phased out or replaced by gods. Of course, women's suffrage was instituted in the United States little more than a half century ago, more than forty centuries after the chivalrous bacchic nations began to fall to our patriarchal forefathers.

Not only was the legal inferiority of women institutionalized, but men and women alike were imprisoned within official, strictly enforced levels of social stratification. These would become the feudal classes in Europe, castes in India, and the enormous body of rules for interpersonal relationships that makes up much of Confucianism.

In the third major characteristic of these patriarchies, while the matriarchal nations were cosmos-oriented and attempted by creative involvement to understand and help nature, the patriarchies put man at the center of the universe. Whether in India or Greece, they worshipped a monarchic pantheon, a make-believe ruling class of superhumanoid gods who were people, but immortal, and had supernatural powers. In China there was the analogous ancestor worship.

Today, of course, and even by 500 B.C. in classic Greece, such characterizations were regarded as cartoons: Superman, -woman, and -child. The pantheon gods were, no doubt, more interesting, complex, and instructive than Spiderman and Snow

37

White, but by our standards not very realistic. Nevertheless, as these and other stories were written down, they became more logical and systematized, eventually evolving into the Hindu and Greco-Roman religions. Above all, the pantheon stood as a model and justification for social stratification on earth.

The Bacchus character was strategically absorbed into this pantheon as an unsavory personage. In India, Shiva became the god of death and destruction. In Greece, Dionysus was portrayed as an alcoholic madman of a god.

Ranked under the gods were the semigod superheroes who performed miracles and supernatural heroic feats. Frequently walking among the gods, or of demidivine origin, these heroes often garnered huge cult followings and, in some cases, were regarded as gods in their own rights. Several hundred years after their deaths, such hero characters would become the symbolic focus of a given patriarchal tribe's imperial state religion, as did the Buddha in India, the Christ in Rome, and the Prophet for the Arabs—messianic god figureheads to whom we will return.

As time passed, the expanding Semitic and Indo-European tribes began to converge and war among themselves, particularly in the Middle and Near East. The expansions and contractions of their power, a seesaw rise and fall of victory and defeat, resulted at one point in the successive Indo-European triumphs we know as the Persian, Greek, and Roman empires, which spanned the millennium from about 500 B.C. to about A.D. 500 And it was during this period that the world would witness a major revival of mystical thought.

Reemergence of Matrio-Mystical Culture

As the world's matriarchal civilizations collapsed militarily, many of their practices, attitudes, and knowledge were forced underground; they were often preserved for centuries within secret societies. This is why, today, we often associate mysticism with the esoteric, arcane, veiled, or hidden. Mystical originally meant "closed," as in sealed lips.

There finally came a time, however, as the patriarchies became more civilized, when mystical ideas about creativity, chivalry, and celebration were able to reemerge and even, beginning about 500 B.C., played an increasingly prominent role in the major cultures of the world.

In Greece, in the full-blown reblossoming of matriarchal attitudes that we call the Golden Age of Classic Greece, the arts, sciences, philosophies, and political principles such as democracy and women's rights burst upon the scene. The most prominent Greek artists and philosophers, such as Plato, wrote frankly about the earlier golden age, from which the accomplishments of classic Greece were derived. But later historians frequently wrote of these accounts as a sentimental, mythological harkening for the good old days, a coverup of matrio-mystical civilization, known as the "classic illusion."

"In all history, nothing is so surprising or so difficult to account for as the sudden rise of civilization in Greece." So marveled a well-meaning Bertrand Russell in his "authoritative" *History of Western Philosophy*. In Greece, the secret transmission of matriarchal attitudes comprised a long series of initiatory exercises known as the mysteries, from which we get the word mysticism. The parallel reemergence of mystical principles in China was what we know as Taoism, and in India, Tantrism. Each would champion personal autonomy and the rights of women, the advance of arts and science, and the celebration of sensual life, including mystical sex.

The later Taoist and Tantric writings on mystical sex were in many ways virtually identical, each describing it in three components: timelessness, spontaneity, and a meditative state of mind. My discussion of mystical sex in chapters 2, 3, and 4 is based on this schema and on the Taoist and Tantric literary commentaries, which are better preserved than their Western counterparts.

From the reflowering of mystical ideas came several syntheses of the basic principles. One such evolving mystical tradition in the Mediterranean world was a Christian mysticism called Gnosticism. There has been speculation as to whether Jesus Christ was espousing mystical ideas. The *Encyclopedia Biblica* tells us, "In the second century, and also to some extent in the third, the church was engaged in a life-and-death struggle with the Gnostics." The deadly conflict between Christianity and Western mystical tradition, often referred to under the umbrella term Gnosticism, would emerge in response to future expressions of mystical themes.

Perhaps the pinnacle of this mystical reemergence was manifested around 300 B.C. in the conquests of Alexander the Great, who carried with him the orientation of classic Greece, and consequently owed much of his success to being welcomed as a liberator by the populations of Egypt, Persia, and India.

To a large extent, mystical principles had gained acceptance, and the popular religions based on the pantheon of gods and ancestor worship lost much of their influence. But some time following Alexander's death there began a gradual and largely conscious effort on the part of governments to withdraw and hide knowledge from the public at large.

About 200 B.C. in China, for example, the government ordered the burning of all books except technical manuals; the classics would be rewritten later by Confucian authorities. About the same time in the West, the flat-earth Ptolemaic map of the world was brought into use, even though sophisticated astronomy had been known for centuries. Libraries were burned, and eventually all universities would close. Gradually, the forces of political, sensual, and creative repression were mobilized for conquest and occupation. Monarchs brought into requisition the superhero model of popular theology, whereby a miracle-working, demidivine savior/protector, accompanied by sacred scriptures and a professional priest class, became the focus of indoctrination, belief, and obedience. Local heroes, usually having died decades or even centuries earlier but still commanding large cult followings, were selected and promoted at politically crucial times. Thus the official, imperial role of Confucianism in China and Buddhism in India around 200 B.C., Christianity in the Roman world about A.D. 300, and Muhammadanism for the Arabs in roughly A.D. 600.

The rise of these religions and the national powers that employed them prefaced centuries of social devolution, superstition, and loss of personal freedom, known in Europe as the Dark Ages. In Europe, this frightful era lasted until mystical principles began reemerging around A.D. 1000, as the various, closely connected movements as Alchemy, Chivalry, and Kabbalism began to grow in influence. For almost three centuries a psychic revolution would spread throughout Europe, emanating from Spain and the south of France, where Christian, Jewish, and Arabic communities coexisted in an increasingly mystical culture.

Throughout Europe, artistic creativity began to flourish, including the cathedral architecture of the Templars and the intricate, complex poetry and love music of the troubadors. The troubadors sang of the love, respect, and even worship of women, establishing the literary themes for what we know as romantic love. As René Nelli, who is regarded as one of the foremost modern interpreters of Chivalry, pointed out in his *Eroticism of the Troubadors*, the troubadors also promoted the notion of mystical sex, exactly as I will describe it.

Scientific and philosophical creativity was also promoted, especially through Alchemy and Kabbalism. Many groups espousing traditional mystical principles began to come together in Europe at this time. Often closely interrelated and mutually supportive, they won the allegiance of populations in numerous cities and regions in every country. Such societies included the many sects of the Cathars and Templars, and later the Brethren of the Free Spirit, Perfectionists, Adamites, Beghards and Beguines, Anabaptists, and other Eleutherians; still later the Rosicrucians, Freemasons, and others.

To counter this movement, the Christian church embarked on a long series of genocidal crusades against the principal centers of mystical (heretical) thought, during which whole cities were burned, including the buildings, books, and inhabitants. In 1209, for example, Pope Innocent III launched a crusade against the Albigensian culture in the south of France; it was "the first genocide or systematic massacre of a people recorded by our 'Christian' western history," as pointed out by Denis de Rougemont, the greatest modern synthesizer of the history and psychology of romantic love, in *Love in the Western World*.

In the fashion of popular theology, science, women, and sensuality were all repressed, and a paranoid superstition was spread by the church's secret police or Inquisition, which executed hundreds of thousands of heretics. The Inquisition's guidebook, the *Malleus Maleficarum*, declared among other things, that "all witchcraft comes from carnal lust, which in women is insatiable." The church was merciless in its attempt to repress truth and freedom; it forbade the printing or even possession of books written in the languages of the people. But as it became widely known that the earth is round and as people began to read, the grip of the church loosened. The final reappearance of mystical social principles came into prominence, signaling what we call the Enlightenment, beginning around 1700.

Modern science, the arts, democracy, women's rights, and the "pursuit of happiness" all gradually came to be heralded. They first blossomed in America and France, and were highlighted by the liberating military campaigns of Napoleon and George Washington. Walt Whitman's poem "One's-self I Sing," from the early nineteenth century, echoes those traditional mystical attitudes toward freedom, nature, and sensuality:

> One's-self I sing, a simple separate person,
> Yet utter the word Democratic, the word En Masse.
>
> Of physiology from top to toe I sing,
> Not physiognomy alone, nor brain alone is
>   worthy for the Muse—I say the
>   Form complete is worthier far,
> The Female equally with the Male, I sing.
> Of life immense in passion, pulse, and power,
> Cheerful, for freest action form'd
>   under laws divine,
> The Modern Man I sing.

The nineteenth century saw a dramatic outburst of mystical orientation, which we can see in the celebration of personal autonomy and self-sufficiency, as described by Eric Thurin in his study in the metaphysics of sex, *Emerson as Priest of Pan.* This thought influenced movements toward democracy throughout Europe and a monumental sexual revolution in America that led to reproductive rights for women, as well as political suffrage. Creatively, the nineteenth century witnessed the overtaking of the church by science as the ultimate arbiter of reality. From Darwin to Einstein mystical ways of looking at the world enjoyed a renaissance and revitalized application to modern life, one dynamic example of which was described by Fritjof Capra in his modern classic, *The Tao of Physics.*

It is on this swing of the pendulum that we find ourselves today. Around the world and within our own culture, we find momentum for and against the themes of mysticism and popular theology. In China and Russia, the people struggle for democracy. In America, the people struggle with the balance between responsibility and the freedom to celebrate and experience altered states of consciousness; one glaring example of this struggle is the "drug problem."

Even today, we are still pulled between the forces of superstition and science. Some Christian leaders actually want the ancient Babylonian myth of the creation of the cosmos, which was later adopted by the Hebrews, taught to children as an "alternative" to scientific theory—the evolutionary equivalent of teaching that the earth is flat as an alternative geography, or the stork theory as a biologic alternative to reproductive anatomy and physiology. The result of this conflict is a seriously misinformed and disinformed populace. Superstition is almost as rampant as ever. In 1988, the National Science Foundation conducted a survey of 2,041 Americans aged eighteen or older. Asked whether the earth goes around the sun or the sun goes around the earth, 21 percent replied incorrectly and 7 percent said they didn't know.

Sexuality remains a focal point in this culture, at the center of our national controversies over abortion, pornography, contraception, sexually transmitted disease, sexual harassment, homosexuality, sex education in school, premarital sex, rape, and other fiercely debated issues. Yet, as organized psychiatry and the churches compete for authority over our sex lives, the mystical attitude is virtually never expressed: that the goal of lovemaking is not procreation, a relief from tension, good health, or even mere pleasure—but a transcendental, altered state of consciousness, or a mystical experience, the result of feeling connected with the cosmos.

Descriptions of Mystical Experience

In his famous work *Varieties of Religious Experience*, American philosopher William James wrote that the "incommunicableness of the transport is the keynote of all mysticism." And, strictly speaking, an altered state of consciousness or mystical experience cannot be definitively described.

Nevertheless, in the various mystical traditions the goal is a transcendental feeling, rather than a conceptual knowledge or belief. For example, as Marvin Meyer revealed in *The Ancient Mysteries*, "Aristotle concludes that the initiates into the mysteries do not learn anything, but rather have an experience and are put in a certain state of mind. . . . They were not given instruction or taught doctrine in any traditional sense."

Inherent in mystical experience itself is the realization that it can't be fully described. That is, achieving this frame of mind helps one to understand the limitations and pitfalls of conceptualization, because mystical experience lies above the verbal, left-mode kind of thinking in terms of labels, definitions, description, and classification.

The incommunicableness of mystical experience also implies the fundamental meaning of secrecy in mysticism, beyond the reference to mysticism's historically being forced underground for survival. It is not that its basic tenets are hidden or otherwise obscure, but that mysticism has no tenets, at least no fixed or inflexible tenets: hence the Taoist saying, "The way that can be spoken is not the permanent way." The implication, furthermore, is that people tend to have a wiser perspective and be more in harmony with nature when they can see through and beyond verbal definitions and other conceptual constructs, and rely instead on feeling and intuition.

Therefore, when we say that we cannot provide a fixed definition of mystical experience, it is not because no one has taken the time and effort needed to describe mystical experience clearly, or because it is too complicated to be summarized succinctly. It is because mystical experience is just that, an experience, which can only be directly, perceptually felt, for the same reason that no verbal description of music can convey the actual sensation of hearing the sounds.

Fortunately, however, there are certain traditional ways in which the mystical state of mind has been alluded to or implied: according to what it is *not*; in simile to other kinds of physical sensations; in spatial and temporal terms; in terms of connection with other things, as a unity or as freedom; in traditionally religious terms; and as limerance, the feeling of being "in love." Again, these are not attempts to delineate or pin down mystical experience, but are intended just to give a hint, a sense, or some flavor of what it is like. Let us take a further look at each of these attempts at describing mystical experience, approaches that often reflect major themes in a broader mystical philosophy.

What Mystical Experience Is Not

First, mystical experience has sometimes been described in terms of what it is *not*: namely, not one of the normal states of consciousness. This is often done by means of prefixes, such as trans-, para-, or supra-, attached to the common human categories of existence: physical, psychological, personal, normal. The mystical experience may be called a paranormal state, a transpersonal plane, a supraphysical sphere of consciousness, transubstantial, or any other combination of such terms. The use of quotation marks and preface words have roughly the same effect, as in "subtle plane" and "true freedom." In this way, what is always emphasized is that mystical experience is outside the ordinary feelings we otherwise know.

Sex through which one attains a mystical state of consciousness is always contrasted with simple, "profane," sensual pleasure. Mystical experience, although achieved during sexual intercourse, is something quite different from the paroxysmal feeling of orgasm, or any other spasmic emotion, no matter how pleasurable. It is different from the instinct for reproduction or from venereal lust. It is different from Kinsey's "outlet," or Freud's "libido" and release from tension, which are not transpersonal, but subpersonal, just as are the stomach, hunger, and visceral satiation.

The erotic impulse, the trauma of coitus, the crisis of orgasm, no matter how good they feel, are all within the sphere of normal, waking consciousness, which we all experience. Hence the Taoist opinion that ejaculation, especially uncontrolled ejaculation, is not the most ecstatic moment, in contrast to what is repeatedly implied or assumed by medical authorities, mass media, and cultural common sense.

On the other hand, mystical experience through lovemaking is not something so vague, fleeting, or ephemeral that it can't be achieved by most people, or isn't already experienced by many and just called by a different name. The saying that "the sensualist is a mystic unawares" implies that people who have a reverent, loving, uninhibited attitude toward their sexual partners may instinctively know what is meant when they hear about mystical sex, as they may already experience sex that way. This saying has also been phrased, "the eroto-maniac is a mystic unawares." But that way of putting it misses the point, and confuses the extended timelessness of coitus reservatus with the insatiable repetition of sex compulsively hunted for by the so-called sex maniac.

Perhaps it should be stressed as this point that, of course, sex is not the only way to achieve an altered state of mind. *Any* activity in which one is timelessly, meditatively, and spontaneously involved can eventually serve the same end, even though many mystical traditions do indeed contend that sexual love provides the easiest, fastest, and most natural method of attaining mystical experience.

Conversely, the altered states achieved in sexual love are among the most frightening and objectionable aspects of sex for the popular theologies. Ideal sex in Christianity, for example, was totally devoid of emotion or feeling. In St. Augustine's classic description, "The husband would be mingled with the loins of the wife without the seductive stimulus of passion, with calmness of mind."

Physical Similarities to Mystical Experience

A second manner of speaking about mystical experience is to compare it in simile to other physiological states. It has been said to be *like* floating, being intoxicated, dazzled; a dizziness or giddiness; a flowing, flying, clear-minded rapture; under a spell, under the influence of a drug or love potion, oceanic, dreamy, trancelike, enchanted, a vibration, a magnetic aura. Of course, if someone describes mystical experience as "dreamy," it doesn't mean that he might have fallen asleep. It means that mystical experience reminded him of, or was somehow *similar* to, that other sensation or consciousness. In this way, the French novelist Balzac mused in *The Physiology of Marriage*, "When, lost in the infinite of my swooning, my soul was separated from my body and hovered far from the earth, I used to think that those pleasures were a means to eliminate matter and to release the spirit to make its lofty flight." If we look at Figure 1, taken from the literature of Alchemy, we see that two lovers are joined sexually. Together, they have a pair of wings, indicating a flying feeling, and the male is in water, insinuating a floating sensation, both sensations that one can be reminded of during mystical experience. A similar, related sensation was discussed by psychologist Mihaly Csikszentmihalyi in his informative book *Flow*.

Spatial and Temporal Comparisons

Mystical experience has also been spoken of in spatial and temporal terms, as height or depth dimension, in contrast to the normal plane of consciousness. Terms such as profound, dis-

Figure 1. This illustration from Alchemy depicts the flying
and floating sensations of mystical sex.

placed, subtle, beyond, even astral awareness, are used. Of course, mystical experience has nothing in particular to do with actual physical dimensions—high, deep, or wide. What is conveyed is its difference from regular daily awareness.

Many commentators have mistakenly believed that in bringing up such terms as immortality, for example, mystics actually intended to live forever. Instead, however, this type of allusion to the mystical plane of consciousness emphasizes that time seems to stand still in such a flowing state of "eternal present," in which there is no future to progress toward. In the immediate present, one experiences rather than conceptualizes, and one lies outside of time, which itself is just another concept. This is why lovers frequently lose track of time.

Modern poet Octavio Paz utilized this allusion—immortality in sexual love—in his *Sunstone*:

> because two bodies, naked and entwined,
> leap over time, they are invulnerable,
> nothing can touch them, they return to the source,
> there is no you, no I, no tomorrow,
> no yesterday, no names, the truth of two
> in a single body, a single soul,
> oh total being . . .

Mystical Experience as Freedom or Connection

Next, mystical experience has been described in terms of boundaries and connection, sometimes as unity, sometimes as freedom. For example, it has been likened to absorption, immersion, being taken over, oneness with the universe (or with God), a true fusion, being cosmically conscious, connected "like an infant holding the breast in its mouth," or like the "cup and the lip." Or, liberated, freed, unrestricted, detached, egoless, with all conditional qualities eliminated. The French novelist

Stendhal wrote, "A higher force, of which I am afraid, took me out of myself and out of reason." (In its original meaning, the word ecstasy refers to "standing outside" one's body.) As a unifying force, breaking through ordinary barriers, mystical experience is sometimes described by combining opposite terms, as in "dazzling obscurity."

In his *Metaphysics of Sex*, Julius Evola, perhaps Italy's leading writer on mysticism in this century, stated, "Here is the key to all the metaphysics of sex: 'Through the Dyad toward the Unity.'" The conjunction of opposites, another major theme in mysticism, suggests that opposites, even "you" and "I," unite, combine, or join, because the mental distinctions that separate things are dissolved when one stops thinking and evaluating in the transcendental state. Through that very direct perception in lovemaking, there is the unmistakable, undeniable fusion with the sexual partner, not just symbolizing one's unity with the universe, but actually making it a literal fact. We're forced to realize that we *are* one with the cosmos. Hence Erich Fromm's commentary in his *Art of Love*, "Erotic love begins in separateness and ends in oneness."

Mystical Experience as Religious

Next, mystical experience has been expressed in terms we ordinarily think of as religious in the popular sense, as a state that is holy, sacred, exalted, supreme, of astral light, a communion with God, anticipation of the absolute, or as prayer or worship. Psychologist Abraham Maslow in *Religions, Values and Peak Experience* discussed how the "peak experiences, naturalistic though they are, could be listed under the heading of religious happenings, or indeed, would have been in the past considered to be only religious experiences." In this way, mystical sex is a very deeply loving, religious experience.

This description does not support the Freudian idea that religion is merely repressed sexuality. Rather, in the words of Alan Watts, the 1960s American philosopher, "Mythology is not sexual, but sexuality is mythological, since the union of the sexes prefigures the transcending of duality, of the schism whereby man's experience is divided into subject and object, self and other."

Mystical Experience and Love

Finally, mystical experience has been spoken of in terms of love. And being in love has been described in many of the same terms as has mystical experience. When one is in love, one is "walking on air," the ego boundaries dissolve, two lovers feel as one, as if their pairing were made in heaven. Their state of mind is certainly not the everyday consciousness that everyone else seems to experience. "Some think of it as madness," Plutarch said. For Plato, being in love was "a divine delirium." Furthermore, being in love is virtually always sexual, or has a predominant sexual component. Psychiatrist-author M. Scott Peck went further in his *The Road Less Traveled* and boldly stated, "The experience of falling in love is a specifically sex-linked erotic experience . . . consciously or unconsciously sexually motivated."

People in love proclaim: I'm in love with you, I'm under your spell, I want to be united with you, to possess you, to embrace you, forever. How romantic! It is not coincidence that Chivalry and the literature of romantic love, begun by the troubadors in the south of medieval France, reflected neo-Gnostic mysticism, which espoused traditional mystical themes.

So it can be said for now that in mystical sex, lovers fall, at least temporarily, in love. They may or may not love each other before or after they make love. They may barely know each other, or they may know each other too well. But as they attain mystical experience together, at least for that moment—or that hour—they can experience the feelings of love.

Of course, there are differences between being in love and mystical sex. A couple can be in love and have a mediocre sex life. A couple can have mystical sex but not otherwise be in love. Furthermore, a chronic history of frequently, uncontrollably falling in love can be the symptom of an underlying emotional problem, as can a history of sexual promiscuity, mystical or otherwise. Still, the connection between mystical sex and being in love, if temporary, is profound, and can have far-reaching consequences for a marriage or relationship.

Finally, these categories or fashions of trying to convey mystical experience overlap and are somewhat interchangeably and indiscriminately used. We could hear of one becoming "free from restrictions," "beyond the physical," in a "depth dimension of vibration and exaltation," all at the same time. Giulano Kremmerz in *Introduzione alla Magia* used a variety of descriptions in speaking of mystical experience as applied to sexual lovemaking:

> To love and desire each other . . . in a continuous
> manner . . . in a state of exaltation that goes on with-
> out any fear of possible zones of dizziness. You will
> feel a sense of real amalgamation; you will feel your
> companion throughout your whole body, not by con-
> tact but in a subtle union that is aware of her at every
> point and pervades her like an intoxication that takes
> possession of the blood of your blood. In the end, that
> takes you to the threshold of a state of ecstasy.

In practice, mystical experience refers to a range of feelings, as does sexual excitement. It can be faint or intense, and typically it seems different each time. But although we are just learning to observe and measure it objectively, it is, for each of us, an unmistakable personal reality. This state of consciousness is real and attainable—best experienced, say many of the mystical traditions, through sexual intimacy.

But how does one go about having mystical sex, lovemaking that leads to this altered state of consciousness called mystical experience? No description of music allows us to hear the actual sounds; but instructions—notes on a musical page—can allow the sounds to be reproduced, and then we can hear it. In the same way, although no description of mystical experience conveys the actual feeling, the mystical literature did provide three basic instructions so that transcendental feelings can be brought about: "contain semen, contain thought, and contain breath." These three injunctions, which refer to the timelessness, meditative state of mind, and spontaneity that characterize mystical sex, and the instructions that will allow us to feel the sensation of mystical experience through sexual lovemaking, are the subjects of the following three chapters.

Three Aspects of Mystical Sex

An enormous portion of the Chinese Taoist and Indian tantric literature from roughly A.D. 200 to A.D. 900, as well as Tibetan and other mystical writings, is devoted to stopping semen, thought, and breath. The idea of stopping or containing so much was not meant to be taken literally, but symbolized three themes of broad application to the mystical traditions. As such, the holding of semen, thought, and breath can be applied to more than just sex. Generally speaking, it can be used as a guide for balancing the two brain hemisphere modes of thinking during any activity. It can be an excellent basis for commentary about mystical sex in particular. Specifically, according to this schema, mystical sex could be seen to have three characteristics: first, as a sort of coitus reservatus (contain semen), it is timeless; second, it is engaged in with a certain meditative frame of mind (stop thought); and third, it is carried out in a spontaneous manner, without having to deliberately do anything at all, as effortlessly as one's breath goes on and on. Chapters 2, 3, and 4 correspond to these three ways of speaking about mystical sex.

Chapter 2 discusses a kind of coitus reservatus, which can be thought of as the physiological aspect of mystical sex. Coitus reservatus is timeless in two ways. First, it is lovemaking that lasts as long as both lovers want, outside any concern or constraint of time or duration. Hence the injunction to contain semen; however, this is not necessarily orgasmless sex, as there is nothing "wrong" with climaxing, except when it causes lovemaking to end before both partners are ready. Second, coitus reservatus lies outside the continuum of time, past or future, because lovers are completely absorbed in the present moment. In fact, it is the absorption in one's immediate feelings that allows for the control of sexual excitement and enables endless lovemaking. Accordingly, chapter 2 will discuss how lovers (especially men) can learn to allow sex to continue indefinitely, a process that was described in detail in the mystical literature, and is identical to that used by modern sex therapists.

Coitus reservatus will be shown to be the easiest and most natural way to make love. It is recommended in the mystical literature not because it prolongs pleasure, but because it maximizes the intimacy and the unity between lovers, and consequently promotes mystical experience.

Chapter 3 describes mystical sex in terms of a meditative state of mind, which could be thought of as the mental aspect of mystical sex. The meditative state of mind referred to in the mystical literature involves the direct experience of physical sensation. It is a right hemisphere mode of thinking or, more precisely, of not thinking. Hence the instruction, contain your thoughts.

This is not a suggestion that one should make love with a blank mind, unaware of what is going on. It means nearly the reverse, that one is more mentally aware and able to get immersed in the experience when one is not flooded with covert self-talk. Chapter 3 will show how this mental approach was promoted by the mystical traditions and will discuss some common patterns of thought that go through people's minds during lovemaking, including examples of psychopathic sexuality, sexual dysfunction, and what psychiatry calls "healthy" sex. Finally, there will be a detailed description of how one goes about "not thinking" during sex, based on both mystical and modern psychotherapeutic techniques.

Chapter 4 discusses mystical sex as spontaneity, which can be seen as the behavioral aspect of mystical lovemaking. In the ancient world, the word breath referred, in addition to its literal meaning, to deliberate action. Therefore, when the mystical literature suggested that one stop breathing, it meant that one should act spontaneously and effortlessly, in the same way that actual breathing automatically goes on and on without one's having to do anything at all. This is why sex advice is bound to miss the point—carrying out instructions for sexual behavior prevents lovers from making love instinctively. Examples of such advice can be found in the *Kama Sutra*, the *Perfumed Garden*, ancient Chinese sex manuals, and modern medical sex therapy resources.

Spontaneity is also a major component in all artistic creativity, whether in drawing, cooking, dancing, playing music, or making love. As with all arts, the how-to of sexual spontaneity is based on a sense of feel and sensation, rather than on following instructions. It has been compared to coasting on a bicycle, which is principally a flowing with the movement, with the rider having to do relatively little.

Finally, chapter 4 will discuss how the three characteristics of mystical sex go together as reflections of a right hemisphere orientation, and how these three components bring about the altered state of consciousness called mystical experience.

Chapter 5 will look at some of the ways mystical attitudes in general and mystical sex in particular can be applied to a male-female relationship. We will look at mysticism's approach to marriage, communication, and morals. We will explore how mysticism is concerned with the tangible aspects of a man-woman partnership—feelings and actions—rather than with marital roles that couples consciously or unconsciously act out, or with what marriage is supposed to be according to law, religion, or tradition.

2

Mystical Sex as Coitus Reservatus

The "innermost secrets" of the Kabbalah are what is "occult" in all occultism: erotic-mysticism and a group of practices of the sort we call yoga. For the Kabbalist the ultimate sacrament is the sexual act, carefully organized and sustained as the most perfect mystical trance.

"Introduction" from A.E. Waite's *Holy Kabbalah*
KENNETH REXROTH

The ancient Chinese believed that ejaculation—especially uncontrolled ejaculation—was not the most ecstatic moment.

The Tao of Love and Sex
JOLAN CHANG

Yoga is an exact science of techniques for controlling processes in the service of specific ends. . . . The mystery of transmutation is found in other secret traditions as well. Taoism knows of it, and the Alchemy of both the East and West often alludes to its techniques. The stopping of the seminal emission is the cause of the displacement of consciousness and, at its ultimate, of transcendence.

The Metaphysics of Sex
JULIUS EVOLA

KIERKEGAARD'S OBSERVATION, "MOST MEN PURSUE PLEA-sure with such breathless haste that they hurry past it," may have no more subtle or relevant application than to sexual love. For this very reason, coitus reservatus (sex that is not inter-rupted by the male's climax) was the single most widely recom-mended aspect of mystical sex in the mystical literature of all cultures. It is described simply by means of the injunction to make love "without emitting semen," or by the recommenda-tion that one fix, hold, contain, stop, interrupt, or stabilize one's semen, or by speaking of sex that is timeless or endless.

Because there is no accidental male sexual release in coitus reservatus, sex is not forced to end. Therefore this type of love-making provides the unhurried sexual *context* that allows lovers to become immersed in the endless immediate present mo-ment, while their bodies spontaneously move together as one.

Lovers ascend to an altered state of consciousness during "endless" mystical sex, not because so many minutes of sex have been chalked up, not because so much friction, tension, or elec-tricity has been generated, but because the issue of duration is no longer a problem. Mystical coitus reservatus therefore does not primarily refer to a particular sexual duration, but to the state of mind during sex, an attitude in which the present mo-ment of sex is an end in itself. Sexual feelings stream spon-taneously and carry lovers along together in the effortless flow of whatever is happening.

Conversely, of course, mental absorption and spontaneity become irrelevant if sex has already ended "prematurely." And it is impossible to be mentally absorbed in the present if one is chronically worried that lovemaking will come to an abrupt end. Coitus reservatus, then, is the framework of mystical sex within which one can have the time it takes to learn to let go of one's covert self-talk commentary and catch on to one's ability to make love spontaneously, freely, and naturally.

Timelessness

Coitus reservatus is timeless in two ways. It lasts as long as both partners want, outside any concern or constraint of time. And it lies outside the continuum of time, past or future, because lovers are completely absorbed in the present. It is this continuous mental and physical immersion in the immediate intimacy of the present moment that promotes mystical experience, whether the transportation of consciousness lasts for a very few or many actual minutes or hours.

In other words, the purpose for allowing sex to last indefinitely is that, as in any art, there is no *future* purpose to achieve in mystical sex other than to be engaged and involved in the here and now. As in dancing, where there are no beginning or end points marked on the dance floor, there is nowhere to go; the whole point is just to be involved. The experience of music is similar; in Alan Watts's words, "When we make music, we don't do it in order to reach a certain point, such as the end of the composition. If that were the purpose of music, then obviously the fastest players would be the best."

Above all, ongoing and open-ended coitus reservatus promotes, perpetuates, and maximizes the intimacy between two lovers. In a sense, it forces lovers to be intimate, and it is mainly because of this closeness, this unity, this intimacy, this fusion, that coitus reservatus, or timelessness in lovemaking, contributes to the rupture of one's ordinary state of consciousness and leads to the experience of a mystical "high."

There is nothing about simply not having an orgasm that promotes mystical experience, and mystical sex is not simply orgasm deprivation. Mystical sex does not preclude lovers climaxing unless doing so brings an unwanted end to lovemaking. It goes without saying that they may have as many climaxes as they want. The point is for lovers to come to an end, one way or another, the way they both want, not to be suddenly, unexpectedly, accidentally interrupted before one or both are ready (except perhaps as a rare surprise for both).

This way of speaking about coitus reservatus can apply equally to men and women, despite the fact that, especially as a contraceptive technique, coitus reservatus usually refers only to men. But there are many women who respond in what is usually thought of as a man's pattern—reaching orgasm within a few minutes, after which sex becomes uncomfortable and must be discontinued, for a while at least.

Society today looks at the female orgasm as the ultimate goal of sex, proof that he is a good lover and that she is responsive. But women's orgasmic responses vary enormously. For example, many women are rarely or never orgasmic during intercourse, while others are multiply orgasmic, some experiencing several, others a virtually unlimited number of coital climaxes. Consequently, the idea of a sort of female "premature ejaculation" has gone unnoticed, and many leading professional texts have boldly asserted that the condition does not exist.

Men generally can reach orgasm more easily than women, so in those not infrequent cases of women who climax once and quickly, the man usually can bring about his own crisis more or less simultaneously. This is a medically approved scenario, typically replete with self-congratulation, glowing, and expansiveness—and who could be blamed for such feelings! But to the extent that sex *must* end, or that it becomes uncomfortable, it inhibits mystical experience, whether it is the male or the female who comes first. Thus, coitus reservatus can apply to both men and women as a means of allowing for the timelessness of mystical sex.

Furthermore, the race—frantic, systematic, random, patient, or otherwise—some couples undergo to perform a simultaneous orgasm, while fun, can often degenerate into a mutual masturbatory employment of each other's genitalia, all the while missing the greater, endless intimacy that can be experienced from start to unhurried, irrelevant finish.

Of course, climaxing too fast is primarily a man's problem. Descriptions of how to control one's sexual excitement so as not to be accidentally carried "over the falls" have been principally directed at men—as in the literature of the mystical traditions, the nineteenth-century birth control literature, and the information of modern sexual therapy, each of which gave the very same prescription for prolonging intercourse.

For women for whom sex does not become uncomfortable or uninteresting after orgasm, there is no reason to refrain from coming to a physical crescendo during lovemaking. Some (especially younger) men can reach a climax and remain erect and able and willing to continue making love, often able to reach another climax. For both, the same principle applies: it isn't the climax that is a problem; it is only a limitation when it forces an unwanted end to lovemaking.

Coitus Reservatus in the Mystical Literature

"Have sex without emitting semen" is the repeated advice in the mystical writings. Let us take a brief look at some examples of the literature on Tantrism, Arabic mysticism, Taoism, Gnosticism, and Chivalry.

Speaking on Tantric yoga, perhaps the world's leading authority, the late Mircea Eliade, writes in *Techniques du Yoga*:

> Tantrism is *par excellence*, a technique, even though it is fundamentally a metaphysic and a form of mysticism. . . . It "wakens" certain occult forces, which slumber within every man, and there, once awakened, transform the human body into a mystical body. . . . It is a means of divinization and hence of integration, final unification, the human function *par*

excellence, that which determines indeed the incessant cycles of births and deaths—sexual function . . . written in a language intentionally secret and ob- scure, in which a state of consciousness is referred to in erotic terms . . . or quite as well the other way round. And this erotic beatitude, obtained by the stoppage not of pleasure, but its physical effect [male orgasm] was resorted to as an immediate experience for entering the Nirvanic state. Thus Tantrism in- cluded the "novelty" of . . . attempting the trans- substantiation of the human body with the aid of an act which in every form of asceticism symbolizes the state *par excellence* of sin and death—i.e., the sexual action . . . sensual pleasure, which is considered to be the sole human experience that can bring about Nirvanic beatitude and the subjection of the senses— in short, a seminal stoppage.

In Arabic mysticism, according to Julius Evola's *Meta-physics of Sex,*

the rule is that the union with the woman is to be performed so that in no case is its normal final end attained, that is, the seed must not be ejaculated. . . . Above all, there was self-control, different from mere resistance to temptation because all the normal phys- ical and psychic conditions of bodily union with a woman were acceptable, nor was there any command- ment to suppress the feelings that are usually aroused therein, with the sole exception that the emission of seed had to be controlled and prevented.

Once one realizes the meaning and role of coitus reser- vatus in mystical lovemaking, it can be seen that an enormous portion of the Taoist literature was presented in ways that not only instruct, but induce, force, trick, tease, or distract couples into simply prolonging lovemaking. For example, the bombastic suggestion that successive episodes of sexual intercourse without male release will produce magic benefits, including, eventually, communication with the gods, can be viewed as an attempt to bolster a couple's interest and motivation in practicing, striving, and attempting to learn to refrain from accidental climax, as in this translation from Ishihara's and Levy's *Tao of Sex*:

> The Yellow Emperor said, "I wish to hear what the effect is like if you move [make love] but do not emit [semen]." Replied the Woman Plain: "If you move but don't emit, then your life-force and vigor are strengthened. If again you move but don't emit, your ears and eyes are sharpened. If a third time you move but don't emit, all sicknesses vanish. If a fourth time you move but don't emit, the five internal organs [the liver, heart, spleen, lungs, and kidneys] are all pacified. If a fifth time you move but don't emit, the blood and veins are replete. If a sixth time you move but don't emit, the waist and back are hardened and strengthened. If a seventh time you move but don't emit, the buttocks and thighs are increasingly invigorated. If an eighth time you move but don't emit, the body begins to glow. If a ninth time you move but don't emit, longevity will not be lost. If a tenth time you move but don't emit, you can communicate with the gods."

This translation is slightly different from the one given by Jolan Chang in his *Tao of Love and Sex*. And the promise of magical results is an example of both the facetious exaggeration and humor of the ancient Chinese, and Taoism's later degeneration into a cult of health. But, above all, such commentary gave couples a direction to go in; the process, the journey, was a key to mystical experience itself: coitus reservatus.

Taoists openly, affirmatively encouraged sexual intercourse. But they used ploys, persuasion, and admonition to ensure that men would "penetrate without emitting," including the tongue-in-cheek warning that there could be serious danger in ejaculating. From *Le Taoism* by Henri Maspéro, a renowned authority on Taoism:

> The madman squanders the most precious fluid of his body in unbridled pleasures and knows not how to save his seminal energy.
> The Yellow Emperor lay with 1,200 women and became immortal; the common people have only one woman each and destroy their own lives.

The Taoist literature also spelled out with unsurpassed clarity the process through which one can learn to control sexual excitement, a procedure essentially identical to that of our best modern sex therapists, as we will see shortly.

It is often mistakenly believed that platonic love or friendship implies nonsexual love. Arthur Evans points out in *God of Ecstasy* that "[Plato's] basic attitude was that sexuality, if it is to be worthily experienced, must be refined, elevated, and purified to a higher level so that it leads one away from the physical to higher realms. In his system of thought the best way to attain this purification is to abstain from actual orgasm."

In the Mediterranean-European mystical tradition, according to Benjamin Walker, author of *Gnosticism*, "In normal heterosexual union, *coitus reservatus* or intercourse without orgasm was advocated. This form of pure forepleasure was meant to capture the sublime eroticism of Adam and Eve before the Fall. Such spiritualized intercourse was known as acclivity."

Then Walker described coitus reservatus, which Gnostics had also called encratism or invigorism:

> Where intimacy with the opposite sex was permitted, but not consummation . . . without succumbing to the climax . . . a man could therefore put himself to

the test by experiencing all the excitement of close contact with a woman . . . penetrating her, but denying himself the relief of orgasm. . . . The conservation of the sperm was seen as important in restoring to man what is diffused, and could best be done through *coitus reservatus*.

The same theme continued into the Middle Ages in the later Gnostic traditions, including the movement called Chivalry, whose poets, or troubadours, extolled "chaste" love. In his *Love in the Western World*, Denis de Rougemont explained how chivalrous chastity, which some writers believed to be nonsexual, actually referred to coitus reservatus: "'Chastity' thus consisted of making love without actually making it, of seeking mystical exaltation and beatitude . . . but with the preservation of that self-mastery from which a lapse might result in an act of procreation."

Later, de Rougemont devoted an appendix to *Tantrism and Courtesy* that showed how, through coitus reservatus, the troubadours sought transcendence in the "joy of desire," in which "the joy becomes the erotic game *par excellence*, which presupposes *amor imperfectus* as a condition for . . . 'pure' joy, that is to say pleasure without procreation."

The later reemergences of mysticism during the Enlightenment also recommended coitus reservatus. Those movements were at times allied with the social reform movement in America, and coitus reservatus became widely publicized as a contraceptive technique and a symbol of women's sexual, and even political, equality in the nineteenth and the early twentieth centuries. Referred to by many names including karezza, dianism, seraphic kissing, and male continence, it was often mentioned in medical and quasi-medical texts on human sexuality, from which today's sex-therapy techniques for self-control were derived.

One good example of this pre-sex-therapy literature is sex researcher R.L. Dickinson's *Control of Conception*, published in

1931, from which the diagram in Figure 2 is taken. This chart depicts the sexual excitement of both the man and the woman during four possible sexual scenarios: "Average Normal Coitus, Quick Emission Without Orgasm for Wife, Withdrawal (Coitus Interruptus), and Coitus Reservatus."

Misunderstandings of Coitus Reservatus

Coitus reservatus was recommended often, clearly, and unmistakably in the mystical literature throughout history, but has been subject to dramatic misrepresentation since the turn of the century by leading translators and authorities on sexology— probably because of the hang-ups and sexual naïveté throughout our culture until recent years, even among the most prominent "scientific" experts. We know from his biographer that the world's leading turn-of-the-century sexologist, Havelock Ellis, was plagued by premature ejaculation throughout his life. And Dutch gynecologist Theodoor van de Veldt, author in 1926 of what is still the world's all-time biggest-selling sex manual, *Ideal Marriage*, stated that

> The desire to prolong the act may lead to excesses and
> abuses. . . . Its habitual employment has great draw-
> backs, and . . . is out of the question for men of the
> white Western races. . . . Physiologically, it must
> be regarded as a real abuse. . . . Therefore, I *must*
> *utter an urgent warning against Karezza* [coitus
> reservatus].

These authors were in most ways very sensitive, thoughtful, learned, and progressive men. But the sexual consciousness of Western society was such that lovemaking that could be continued indefinitely was simply not considered a possibility by the majority of adults. In a 1931 study of 362 men, Dickinson

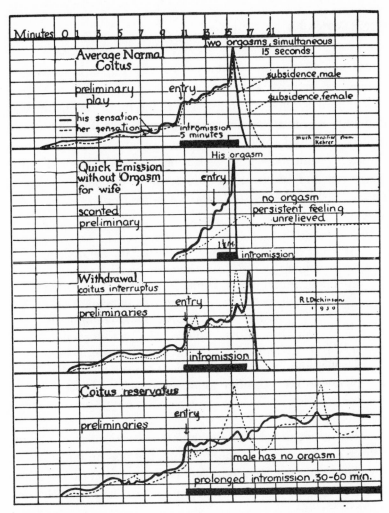

Average Normal Coitus: intercourse lasts about five minutes, ending after both partners reach climax.
Quick Emission Without Orgasm for Wife: intercourse lasts about 1½ minutes, with climax only for the man.
Withdrawal: the woman reaches orgasm, then the man withdraws before he reaches climax.
Coitus Reservatus: intercourse lasts indefinitely, with more than one orgasm for the wife, if desired. The man is exercising control, with his excitement increasing and decreasing, without ever reaching the threshold level.

Figure 2. Several turn-of-the-century American writers, in loose conjunction with the early women's movement, began to emphasize coitus reservatus. The chart from R.L. Dickinson's 1931 *Control of Conception* is a good example of how it was defined and depicted in the first half of the twentieth century, prior to the invention of sex therapy.

found that 12 percent ejaculated "instantly" upon intromission, another 28 percent within three minutes, and another 33 percent within five to ten minutes. Perhaps more significant was that only 3 percent of the men surveyed said that they could control their excitement sufficiently so that they could reach a climax any time they chose, as is more or less the point in coitus reservatus and mystical sex. Much more famous was Alfred Kinsey's 1948 report, *Sexual Behavior in the Human Male*, which revealed:

> At lower educational levels, it is *usual* for the male to try to achieve an orgasm *as soon as possible* after effecting genital union. Upper level males more often *attempt* to delay orgasm. *For perhaps three-quarters of all males, orgasm is reached within two minutes* after the initiation of the sexual relation, and for a not inconsiderable number of males the climax may be reached within less than a minute or even within ten or twenty seconds after coital entrance [emphasis added].

This unfortunate attitude toward coitus reservatus was not restricted to the professional literature, but was an integral part of Western cultural consciousness, as we can see reflected in the following excerpt from D.H. Lawrence's 1928 classic novel, *Lady Chatterly's Lover*:

> Connie found it impossible to come to her crisis before he had really finished his. And he roused a certain craving passion in her, with his little boy's nakedness and softness; she had to go on after he had finished, in the wild tumult and heaving of her loins, while he heroically kept himself up, and present in her, with all his will and self-offering, till she brought about her own crisis, with weird little cries.

When at last he drew away from her, he said, in a bitter, almost sneering voice:

"You couldn't go off at the same time as a man, could you? You'd have to run the show!"

This little speech, at the moment, was one of the shocks of her life. Because that passive sort of giving himself was so obviously his only real mode of intercourse.

"What do you mean?" she said. . . .

She was stunned by this unexpected piece of brutality, at the moment when she was glowing with a sort of pleasure beyond words, and a sort of love for him. Because after all, like so many modern men, he was finished almost before he had begun. And that forced the woman to be active. . . .

Sex and a cocktail: They both lasted about as long, had the same effect, and amounted to about the same thing.

Writers and translators who worked prior to the revolution in sexual consciousness in the 1960s generally did not see sex without end as a realistic possibility. As late as 1965, in his book *Love and Orgasm*, the popular psychiatrist-author Alexander Lowen warned that "The prolongation of forepleasure activities for the sake of the excitement they provide is not without its danger."

Authors such as Evola and de Rougemont could write impressive—in fact, brilliant—books related to the transcendental issues of sexual mysticism, but did not seem to take seriously the practice of coitus reservatus. Although Evola clearly states in *The Metaphysics of Sex*, "The stopping of seminal emission is the cause of the displacement of consciousness," practically in the same breath he hedged: "Hindu Tantric writings and also Chinese Taoist books should be taken with a grain of salt. . . . It is hard to conceive of a man attaining such a state without isolating himself completely from any erotic stimulation . . . and turn everything into a rather insipid exercise of skill." The message: This is all well and good on paper, but men can't really make love as long as they want. He even included one section entitled "Tantric Sexual Practices and Their Dangers."

De Rougemont alludes to coitus reservatus as "an abstruse psycho-physiological technique" and a "heroic trial." And it can be seen in the literature that almost all the most scholarly modern authors on the subject of mysticism and its sexual components inevitably comment to the effect that the mystical writings prescribe an odd, curious, or contradictory "mixture of sexual restraint and lewd excess." The *Encyclopedia Biblica*'s essay on Gnosticism remarked on sexual attitudes in which "asceticism sometimes changes into wild libertinage." Writing on Taoism, Herrlee Creel remarked on "sexual practices which curiously combined license with austerity." But this was not a mixture at all; what was being clearly, affirmatively recommended was coitus reservatus: extended lovemaking (criticized as libertinage/license) uninterrupted by accidental male emission (mistakenly called asceticism/austerity).

Coitus Reservatus as the Most Natural Way to Make Love

Having lectured for years in the human sexuality sequence of the University of Michigan Medical School, and at professional conferences in America and abroad, I have seen, even among learned doctors and sexual health practitioners, a widespread sense of incredulity at the notion that one can significantly control one's sexual excitement so that lovemaking actually can last indefinitely. In a sense, such misunderstandings about coitus reservatus are part of a bigger cultural myth about sex: specifically, the notion that if one allows one's body to move spontaneously and to experience all the feelings and sensations involved in lovemaking, that one (especially a man) will climax involuntarily. In other words, that coming to an orgasmic end is somehow easier or more natural than making love indefinitely, and, consequently, that coitus reservatus involves a kind of fight against this natural force, a holding off, an inhibition, a struggle of sorts, in order for lovers to continue making love.

The image that coming to a sexual climax is easier or more natural than not coming is rooted in some of our most influential religious and medical theories. However, upon inspection and analysis, these myths show themselves to make little sense.

First was the traditional Christian idea that sex was, without exception, for procreation only. Until a few years ago, the ideal Christian copulatory act was a prompt, impassive fertilization of the ovum. In St. Augustine's words:

> The sexual members, like all the rest, would be moved by the command of the will, and the husband would be mingled with the loins of the wife without the seductive stimulus of passion, with calmness of mind and with no corruption of the innocence of the body. . . . Because the wild heat of passion would not activate those parts of the body, but as would be proper, a voluntary control would employ them.

Sex for any other reason was considered contrary to nature; a quick insemination was seen as the only natural way to make love. For this reason, masturbation was a more serious sin than rape, because in rape there was at least the chance of pregnancy.

In its emphasis on the climax as the goal, the Christian attitude on sex was analogous to that of Freud, who preached that orgasm is the only really pleasurable part of sex; one should achieve it quickly in order to be in sync with nature's "pleasure principle." In *Freud: The Mind of the Moralist*, Phillip Reiff crystallized Freud's image of sex as essentially degrading and dirty. Freud thought of sexual tension as one might think of the urgency to urinate, which is unpleasant:

> In the third of the *Three Essays on Sexuality*, Freud stresses that sexual excitement, because it is a form of tension, must be "Counted as an unpleasurable feeling": Only the act of discharge is acknowledged as a genuine pleasure; the mutual caresses, however pleasant, which precede orgasm are purely anticipatory, the "forepleasure" essentially unpleasant unless quickly surpassed.

This hydraulic Freudian image of orgasm as a letting off of steam carried over into Kinsey, who called it an "outlet" in his charts and text, and to Masters and Johnson, who called it a "release" from "vasoconcentration and myotonia."

But Freud was surely off the mark in his assertion that prolonging sex would be acting contrary to a so-called pleasure principle. It is clear that all that comes before orgasm is a rather obvious pleasure, which, if uninterrupted, will lead couples beyond mere pleasure to love and mystical experience. Any ending to sex is an end to the experience, the intimacy, the pleasure; therefore, by Freud's own reasoning, coming to an end is contrary to a pleasure principle. Certainly, in this sense, it is much more naturally reinforcing and thus easier to continue making love than to end it.

Of course, we must be especially careful of the idea that prolonged sex is good merely because it prolongs pleasure. Such an attitude could only foster what Evola called today's "abstract and vicious hunt for venereal pleasure as a drug and liminal soothing agent."

Kinsey, after finding that three-quarters of the men he surveyed reached a climax within two minutes, apologized for these men in a footnote, stating that such a quick male response was an aid to mankind's evolutionary survival of the fittest—and, therefore, more natural. But this assertion that a rapid ejaculation was an evolutionary advantage to fertility is as far-fetched a notion as saying that cannibalism is an evolutionary aid to nutrition. There is no positive correlation whatsoever between fertilization and the duration of coitus. In fact, there may be a distinct evolutionary advantage to unhurried lovemaking: even a cavewoman would be much more likely to want to mate with a Neanderthal who knew how to make love. By this evolutionary reasoning, it is more likely that men who prolonged sex would be fittest, and would have more naturally survived through the millennia of human development.

Even psychiatrist/sex therapist Helen Singer Kaplan proclaimed that the crucial aspect of premature ejaculation was the absence of "voluntary control over the ejaculatory reflex." This is not only an oxymoron (a reflex being a reaction which by definition must occur involuntarily), but it reiterates St. Augustine's injunction that a "voluntary control" be exerted over the sexual members—bringing full circle the myth that, unless held in check, the natural course of sexual events involves an automatic, involuntary orgasmic climax.

The assertion of sex therapists that men need to exert control over the ejaculatory reflex by means of sex-therapy "techniques" is entirely phony and misguided, as we are about to see. The reason that 98 percent or virtually all men (even chronic premature ejaculators) can learn to make love indefinitely, is that coitus reservatus is a much easier and more natural way to make love than forcing sex to a hasty ending.

According to the mystical literature, mystical sex is not only timeless, but spontaneous and mentally absorbing as well. Essentially, it says that if one lets one's body move freely, while concentrating on the direct perception of feelings and sensations, coitus reservatus will naturally occur. Conversely, it is

75

deliberate effort, pushing oneself to move according to a conceptual idea of how one ought to make love, that brings about a sudden sexual climax. Hence, the treatment of premature ejaculation, or the way to coitus reservatus, to timeless, endless lovemaking, involves the cessation of those deliberate actions that bring on an unwanted climactic release. Let us turn now to look at this simple and virtually always successful procedure.

The How-to of Coitus Reservatus

The behaviors that lead to endless lovemaking are certainly not a formula for "how to make love," nor is coitus reservatus all there is to experiencing mystical sex. The issues of mental absorption and behavioral spontaneity will be addressed in the following two chapters. Nevertheless, being able to make sexual intimacy last as long as lovers want it to is a prerequisite for mystical sex.

Certainly, a lot of men can make love more or less as long as they wish, and a lot can't. What follows is a description of how one can learn to practice coitus reservatus.

The actual process through which one can learn the ability to make timeless love is incredibly simple, and involves only one primary instruction. This basic sexual recipe is that one proceed at a low level of both excitement and stimulation, stop or slow what he is doing if he becomes too excited, then resume after he has calmed down. If a man merely follows this approach, he will eventually catch on to the ability to raise or lower his sexual excitement, so that he never reaches that point at which he climaxes involuntarily. Thereby, he will be able to prolong intercourse more or less indefinitely, experiencing endless closeness and intimacy with his lover.

This "plan" has been found in preserved documents from remote eras and cultures, including the Taoism of ancient

China, the nineteenth-century American social-reform movement, and modern sex therapy. Comparing these texts reveals that those directions are essentially identical, despite the fact that the purpose of coitus reservatus was different for each group. For sex therapy, it is the cure of a psychiatric disorder; for the American social-reform movement it was a contraceptive technique and a generator of social magnetism between man and woman as equals; for Taoism and the other mystical traditions it promoted mystical experience and, thereby, mystical sex.

In his *Tao of Love and Sex*, Jolan Chang translated the second-century Taoist version of this plan:

> The beginner is advised not to get too excited or
> excessively passionate. . . . He should first try the
> method of three shallow and one deep thrust . . . and
> carry out the thrusts eighty-one times as a set. . . . If
> he feels that he is becoming a little excited he should
> stop the thrusting motion immediately. . . . He
> should wait until he has calmed down then resume
> again . . . with the same three shallow and one deep
> method. . . . At last he can try nine shallow and one
> deep. In learning how to control ejaculation one must
> avoid being impatient. . . . The important point to
> remember is that he must retreat when he has just
> become excited . . . it is much better to retreat too
> early than too late.

In *Male Continence*, nineteenth-century American John Humphrey Noyes advised that a man can enjoy the motions of intercourse while stopping short of orgasm.

> We begin by *analyzing* the act of sexual intercourse. It
> has a beginning, a middle, and an end. Its beginning
> and most elementary form is the simple *presence* of
> the male organ in the female. Then usually follows a

series of *reciprocal motions.* Finally this exercise brings on a nervous action or ejaculatory *crisis* which expels the seed. Now we insist that this whole process, up to the very moment of emission, is *voluntary,* entirely under the control of the moral faculty, and *can be stopped at any point.* In other words, the *presence* and the *motions* can be continued or stopped at will, and it is only the final *crisis* of emission that is automatic or uncontrollable. . . .

Suppose the man chooses . . . to enjoy not only the simple *presence,* but also the *reciprocal motion,* and yet stop short of the final crisis . . . a man, knowing his own power and limits, should not even approach the crisis. . . . I *know* that it is possible—nay, that it is easy. . . .

The situation may be compared to a stream in the three conditions of a fall, a course of rapids above the fall, and the still water above the rapids. The skillful boatman may choose whether he will remain in the still water, or venture more or less down the rapids or run his boat over the fall. But there is a point on the verge of the fall where he has no control over his course . . . [E]xperience will teach him the wisdom of confining his excursions to the region of easy rowing, unless he has an object in view that is worth going over the falls.

Contemporary psychiatrist Helen Kaplan in *The New Sex Therapy* describes the standard twentieth-century medical approach:

The patient is told to focus his attention exclusively on the erotic sensations emanating from his penis while he is being stimulated. . . . Thrusting stops when the preorgastic level of sensation is reached. At this point the penis remains in the vagina until the sensation disappears, at which time thrusting is resumed.

In a way, this time-tested technique for learning to practice coitus reservatus is such obvious common sense that it is hardly a technique at all. Furthermore, the basic injunction does not give one control, but it does ensure that lovemaking will continue so that one can find, develop, realize, or discover the ability to control his excitement.

In fact, men who "naturally" are able to prolong intercourse reveal upon careful questioning that they intuitively used this procedure during adolescence or early adulthood to learn control of their sexual excitement. This is perhaps the most important proof that the process of learning control can be quite natural and spontaneous, and need not be mechanical, clinical, or forced.

Incidentally, in a research study on prostitution, psychotherapist Martha Stein found that a large percent of men who visit prostitutes do so for help with premature ejaculation, and that these sexually experienced women utilized this same stop-start method when helping men with that problem.

The Basic Plan as I would describe it to my own clients expands on these instructions:

✦ Alone or with a partner, begin by doing whatever you want (foreplay, intercourse, or self-stimulation), but in SLOW MOTION. Breathe in slow motion. Kiss in slow motion, or no motion. Approach the whole experience so very gradually that you don't even begin to get close to the end.

✦ Avoid a loss of control by stopping. Any time you think you might be nearing climax, stop, or slow down what you're doing. If necessary, discontinue all movement and stimulation. (The secret is to stop as far in advance as you can, *not at the last moment.*)

✦ Any time you stop or slow down, breathe easily, relax, and wait until you calm down. Take plenty of time to wait until you're fully relaxed. At first you may have to spend much of your time lying totally motionless. That's O.K.

✦ Once you become comfortable and relaxed, resume again, doing anything you want but perhaps more slowly and carefully. When you feel that you are in control at a very low level of excitement and stimulation, you may gradually increase your activity. Increase your movement or stimulation just slightly, making sure you maintain control. Keep in mind exactly how excited you are, and stop whenever you become too excited.

✦ Continue stopping and starting as needed, and try to go so slowly you never have to stop, but always do stop well before you think you might be nearing the point of no return.

✦ Persistently and patiently practice this prescription and you will experience more and more time and freedom of activity without ever nearing that fateful moment. Carry out this exercise plan for about a half hour to an hour, alone or with a partner (during foreplay or intercourse), about three to five days each week, for about four to six weeks. Many men require even less time than that to learn control.

Figure 3 shows the Basic Plan in simple form. It is based on the "test-operate-test-exit" structure of plans devised by George Miller et al., in their *Plans in the Structure of Behavior.*

Three critical issues, often overlooked by even the best-intentioned psychologists and authors on human sexuality, are sometimes confusing for men or women learning to practice coitus reservatus. Those critical issues in learning to control one's sexual excitement are: (1) it doesn't matter what sexual behavior is engaged in, as long as one stays in the sexual milieu; (2) one should slow down or discontinue stimulation long before nearing a climax (not at the last moment); and (3) one does not seek to control his climax directly, but controls his level of excitement so that he doesn't reach that point at which his climax occurs reflexively. Let us now look at these three points in greater detail.

Anything Goes

It doesn't matter what sexual behavior one engages in when learning coitus reservatus. Foreplay, intercourse, or self-

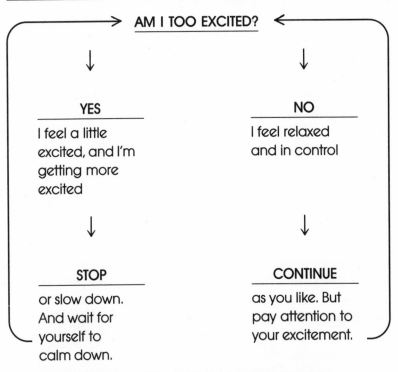

AM I TOO EXCITED?

YES	NO
I feel a little excited, and I'm getting more excited	I feel relaxed and in control

STOP	CONTINUE
or slow down. And wait for yourself to calm down.	as you like. But pay attention to your excitement.

Figure 3. The Basic Plan is the idea you keep in mind as you gradually recondition your body's sexual response pattern during foreplay, intercourse, or self-stimulation.

stimulation are all appropriate. Furthermore, it is helpful to get away from the idea that there is a beginning, a middle, and an end through which sex progresses.

All sexual experiences can be seen as reconditioning or relearning opportunities, and in fact, every sexual experience does influence one's future sexual pattern, whether one wants it to or not. For example if a man masturbates in a hurried fashion with orgasm as the goal and purpose, that approach will carry over into and speed up his sexual response with a partner. For the same reason, and contrary to what many men think, the longer a man spends in foreplay, the longer intercourse will tend to last as well, since foreplay is just another way for someone to learn an endless sexual pattern.

Today's most popular sexual psychology texts often contain the mistaken and unnecessary suggestion that to learn self-control a man must gradually proceed in a regime of numerous steps, or different sexual reconditioning-exercise episodes, over a period of days, weeks, or months, beginning with easier or less anxiety-provoking sexual behaviors, and progressing toward intercourse (as if intercourse were the most "difficult" sexual activity). This progression typically begins with an injunction that a couple engage in a nonsexual body massage: Masters and Johnson called this "sensate focus"; Hartman and Fithian called it a "caress" exercise. The next time they are intimate, the couple is told to change to a sexual massage but without lubrication; the time after that, the couple is instructed to perform a sexual massage with a nonallergenic oil or lotion. The lovers then proceed through further intermediary steps toward intercourse—first with the woman on top, as that is generally deemed less stressful!

Hartman and Fithian in *The Treatment of Sexual Dysfunction*, for example, recommended that couples begin the treatment process by giving a foot massage to each other.

> We perceive a close positive correlation between the
> premature ejaculator and the fast foot caress . . .
> SLOW—SLOW—SLOW is one of the main suggestions
> we must make. . . . If it feels good, take time to en-
> joy it. . . . It generally takes an hour to an hour and a
> half to complete the Foot Caress. . . . It is not unusual
> to have one or both a bit teary at this point, especially
> where touch between them has been taboo for a
> period of months or years.

I have nothing at all against a foot caress, a nonsexual massage, or foreplay of any kind. In fact, I highly recommend them all, whether or not they lead to intercourse and/or a climax of some sort. But it's not *necessary* for a man to begin with, or avoid, or proceed toward or from those or any other particular sexual positions or behaviors. The only important qualification is that lovers stay in the sexual situation.

Furthermore, overly specific sex instructions make the whole learning process much more awkward, in the same way that footprints painted on the floor make learning to dance unnatural. In his otherwise fine book, *Male Sexuality*, therapist Bernie Zilbergeld lapsed into this dictatorial motif, with ordered, numbered exercises, some with steps, and often according to various additional guidelines:

> Do the exercises in the order in which they are
> presented. . . . If the next exercise gives you a lot of
> trouble and the situation does not improve after
> several attempts, go back to the previous one until
> you are more comfortable with it. . . . EXERCISE
> 15-1: STOP-START MASTURBATION. *Step A*: With a
> dry hand (no lotion or other
> lubrication). . . . EXERCISE 15-2: MASTURBATING
> WITH SUBTLE ADJUSTMENTS. . . .
> Many men . . . will want to move on to partner sex.
> They should first, however, do the last exercise in this

series, 15-5. . . . It is crucial that you have mastered
the exercises in Chapter 15. . . . EXERCISE 16-3:
PENIS IN VAGINA WITH NO MOVEMENT. . . .
EXERCISE 16-5: USING DIFFERENT POSITIONS FOR
INTERCOURSE. . . .

The tendency to put learning into graded steps was a holdover from a fashion in the treatment of various problems, sexual
problems among them, used by behavior therapists whose techniques were evolving and coming into vogue in the 1950s and
1960s. Sex therapy, as an area of specialization within behavior
therapy, became so highly visible and claimed to be so successful that it branched off as a separate field around 1970. It lost
touch with an enormous body of research data from behavior
therapy, which revealed among other things that a hierarchic
approach to desensitization is unnecessary. In fact, as a valid
theory, the birth, life, and death of systematic desensitization
had been well detailed by the early 1970s, but somewhat unconsciously, sex therapy held over the primitive, step-by-step, now-
do-this/now-do-that approach to its treatment instructions.

Influenced by this superstition, my 1975 self-help booklet
broke the treatment of premature ejaculation into fourteen
days' worth of exercises, each with numerous steps, conditions,
time frames, explanations, and a precise order. The program
included an anatomic self-examination; a performance and
identification of the four stages of sexual response; various aspects, phases, twists, and possibilities of male sexual response
(involving a manual squeeze of the penis, the stop-start procedure, the sexual muscles, the Cowper's gland secretion, and
partial/sequential "multiple" ejaculations). Then the partner exercises, foot/face/body/sexual massages, and several modes and
positions of intercourse! Whew!

After clinically testing all the many steps—that is, by having patients who complained of premature ejaculation go
through that program—I soon realized that the only thing that

mattered was that the man follow the basic instruction plan of learning to control his excitement level, regardless of what he was doing. Once that orderly, precise style of treatment proved unnecessary, it was possible to see that there was no need for the exceedingly clinical, sterile approach to sex that has been unconsciously projected by today's professionals.

The fact that a man or woman who wants to learn to control his or her sexual excitement need not adhere to a strict series of specific behaviors is obviously a relief to the many people without partners, or with only marginally cooperative partners, as they can use self-stimulation. This approach is of equal usefulness to those who, on the other hand, are opposed to masturbation (as many authorities insist on masturbation as a first step). In the same way, it is workable for partners who wish to help, but who may be uncomfortable with certain sexual behaviors in general or at various times.

He Who Hesitates Will Last

It is easiest to learn to practice coitus reservatus at a low level of sexual excitement because it is easier to learn to control one's excitement at a lower level. Therefore, during lovemaking, one stops and waits to calm down or changes what he's doing in order to diminish sexual stimulation long before he approaches the climax. Stimulation is reduced or entirely discontinued long before the "point of no return," which Masters and Johnson called the feeling of "ejaculatory inevitability." For men, that sensation accompanies the phase of the orgasm during which the semen flows from the prostate gland and seminal vesicles into the urethral bulb at the base of the penis, just prior to its being automatically ejaculated.

If man engages in sex at a high level of arousal, he will not recondition his sexual response pattern as quickly, and will

85

simply find it much more difficult to learn self-control than if he makes love at a lower level of excitement. Many men report that if they reach a certain high level of sexual excitement, and then discontinue stimulation and wait to calm down, they quickly return to that very high, uncontrollable level once stimulation is resumed. Whereas, if one begins to learn control at a relatively low level of excitement—and increases his excitement only as fast as his control will allow, eventually he will be able to enjoy those very high levels of excitement—and low levels, and medium levels, and any combination or variety he chooses, without losing control.

The slow-motion, low-level-of-excitement approach is used temporarily at first, because this is the best way to catch on to the ability to control sexual excitement at any level. A misunderstanding of this point led many turn-of-the-century commentators to conclude that coitus reservatus was somehow motionless sex. In fact, they had confused coitus reservatus with the *process of learning* to practice spontaneous, uninhibited lovemaking.

Furthermore, if a man tries to learn sexual self-control at a high level of arousal, there is the danger that the experience will be interrupted entirely by accidental ejaculation. In terms of learning to control his excitement, the man will find that with ejaculation and the refractory period, there is simply no excitement to learn to control. Which is why the sooner the man stops or slows down, the better. As the Taoists advised, "Better too early than too late."

To be sure, the sexual experience does not necessarily end with the man's climax. Lovers can continue to caress each other, maximize body contact, enjoy closeness and intimacy; they can talk; the partner may want to be further satisfied in some way; about the last thing one would be advised to do is to leave the room or roll over and fall asleep.

The instruction to stop or slow down what he's doing before he gets too excited means that the man should *change* something so that he does not get more excited. Although for most men, simply slowing down or stopping whatever they're doing is the best way to achieve this, some men report that in certain situations, slowing down is more of a turn-on; when they slow down, they have less self-control. In a similar way, it is occasionally reported that stopping completely can be more exciting than slowing down. Therefore, before one gets too excited, he may want to consider a change of positions, a change in the type of sexual stimulation, a change of where the bodies make contact, a change in the rhythm of the movement or in some other factor. These are very personal and individual issues, and the man can stay aware of what works best for him and his partner if he proceeds slowly, and carefully stays in touch with his feelings all along the way.

It is with regard to this issue—that one reduces stimulation well before the point of no return—that we can see perhaps the single biggest mistake today's psychologists make in treating premature climax: encouraging men to practice brinksmanship and approach orgasm when learning to control their sexual excitement. This unfortunate oversight may be so widespread because, beginning with Masters and Johnson, most psychiatric authorities have believed that the basic treatment instructions were invented by a urologist actually named James Semans, who wrote an article in 1956 for the *Southern Medical Journal* entitled, "Premature Ejaculation: A New Approach." In that article, the author advised the man to stop when he felt the "sensation premonitory to ejaculation."

Waiting until the "sensation premonitory to ejaculation" is waiting too long, but this oversight carried over into all the subsequent works on this subject. For example, in the book many consider the single most important sexual therapy text, *The New Sex Therapy*, Kaplan, after recommending the obligatory preliminary steps, gave her instructions, which she called a variation of Semans's, recommending one stop at the "preorgastic" level of excitement.

A question arises as to why anyone would accept Semans as the originator of the basic method. Semans's lone bibliographic reference, *Power to Love* by Edwin Hirsch, published in 1934, was only one of many quasi-medical works over the previous hundred years, including turn-of-the-century feminist literature, which described the basic instruction plan in one degree of clarity or another.

The ancient Taoist as well as nineteenth-century American descriptions of the basic procedure did not make the mistake of recommending brinksmanship. Instead they suggested not getting too excited, and confining oneself to Noyes's "area of easy rowing," rather than the "point on the verge of the fall."

Having made such a point of this, I should add that there is absolutely nothing wrong with having sex at a preorgastic, highly aroused condition. One can even play games with oneself and one's partner, such as approaching a climax so closely and so gradually that involuntary contractions begin, but stopping just short of orgasm itself. Or the man can go a tiny bit further and allow only a partial emission and ejaculation. Repeated sequentially, this gives the appearance of so-called multiple male orgasms, which Hartman and Fithian have documented on film. I even recommended such antics myself when I first studied the treatment of premature ejaculation. It's all well and good, but it just doesn't help a man learn coitus reservatus.

There is also nothing "wrong" with intense levels of sexual stimulation, whether in terms of friction, pressure, lubrication, tension, rapidity of movement, direction of movement, or any other physical or mental factor or combination of factors. I'm certainly not against any of that. But it's silly for someone to be stimulated intensely if it causes the experience to end abruptly, suddenly, and uncontrollably; and it is pathetic, to requote D.H.

Lawrence, if that is "his only real mode of intercourse." So, in beginning to learn sexual self-control, some men should use just barely enough stimulation to maintain an erection.

The suggestion that one move little or not at all does not apply only to those men who ejaculate very rapidly. It is part of a broader picture in which lovers do not make forced or deliberate movements but allow their bodies to spontaneously move of their own accord, by a sense of feel. In fact, if one does nothing at all, that is, makes no premature effort to "shuck and jive" in some preconceived way, but only allows himself to perceive directly all the feelings and sensations of making love, his body will eventually begin to move in a much more sensuous, natural, and spontaneous way. At the same time, this keeps him from reaching that point at which he climaxes involuntarily, because it is principally purposeful motion—usually the "hard-driving fuck," or a variation thereof—that brings about an uncontrollable climax, and at which the injunction to slow down too soon rather than too late is directed.

A lack of attention to this issue is a major reason why today's psychotherapists report that the procedure needs to be practiced for six months to a year. In fact, properly carried out, it takes only a few weeks or less for a man to recondition his sexual response pattern and learn to control his sexual excitement. Ancient Taoists said it could be done in ten days or less. I would estimate that for most men it takes less than twenty-four hours: four hours per week for six weeks, or three hours per week for eight weeks, and so forth.

Journey of a Thousand Miles

The third point in learning to practice coitus reservatus is that one learns to recognize and control the stage of his overall sexual excitement, not the orgasm or ejaculation itself. One controls whether he is getting less or more excited so as not to reach that point at which orgasm occurs by reflex; he does not look for a direct switch or trigger to turn his climax on or off once he is at that point.

Once a man gets in touch with his ability to raise or lower his excitement, then he can automatically do it by feel. Sort of like riding a bicycle, it becomes second nature. One finds that it is more natural and easier to maintain the intimate unity of lovemaking than to push oneself "over the falls."

The ability to practice coitus reservatus, then, comes from being aware of one's feelings, not from repressing, blocking, or ignoring them. This point is well-illustrated in the following story, which appeared in Marc Fasteau's valuable book, *The Male Machine*.

> Three minutes and it was all over, despite his best intentions and efforts. He couldn't do anything about it until he realized that he was so concerned about orgasm—hers, his, the timing—that he was paying no attention to what he was feeling. When he began to think of these emotions and sensations not merely as way stations but as experiences to be enjoyed for their own sake, two changes occurred: He became more acutely aware of what he was feeling, making it possible for him to *slow the rate of stimulation temporarily and lower his level of sexual excitement whenever he felt himself approaching premature climax.* But, equally important, the act of focusing positively on these feelings, their nuances and variations, and on the accompanying initiatives and responses, dissolved what had been an unconscious haste to end it. The premature ejaculation stopped. He had discovered a basic paradox of human behavior—*trying to ignore, to "conquer" feeling leads not to more self-control and freedom but to less* [emphasis added].

The more one is fully absorbed in the feelings and sensations of lovemaking, the more easily one may practice coitus reservatus. Not only will he better know when to stop or slow down, but it is the spontaneous, immediate feedback of sensation that allows him to raise or lower his sexual excitement.

For psychologists, this issue is the most misunderstood aspect of the learning procedure. They misguidedly assert that men should somehow control their ejaculatory reflexes directly, and that by pausing and waiting to calm down, the man gains control. In fact, pausing and calming down have nothing in particular to do with gaining voluntary control of sexual excitement, except that they prevent the sexual learning experience from ending. Furthermore, some authors such as Kaplan have stated that the man practicing the procedure should make four pauses before ejaculating; others, such as Zilbergeld, say three. The number of pauses is completely irrelevant, whether they are very few or very many.

What's even more misleading is the medical insinuation that certain other maneuvers, or squeeze techniques, somehow give the man self-control; they do *not*. There is nothing "wrong" with, and I have nothing *against* squeezes, maneuvers, or anything else done by the man or his partner to learn more about their sexuality, get further in touch with their sexual response patterns, just for fun, to tease, to gain confidence, as a source of intimacy, as a surprise, for variety, to improve communication, or for any other reason. It's just that they are not particularly helpful to a man learning to practice coitus reservatus.

Why the Basic Plan Works

There are several ways in which the basic procedure enables men or women to practice coitus reservatus. Some of these mechanisms are easy to explain, others are elusive. For example, it is easy enough to see that simply remaining in a sexual situation for extended periods of time will help increase self-control on a purely physiological level. Sexual anxiety, worry, and nervous tension will abate with prolonged exposure to the sexual scene. In addition, the man's physical sensitivity (or, more correctly, reactivity) to physical or mental stimulation is diminished, and the threshold level at which his climax occurs reflexively is actually significantly raised, so that much more stimulation is required before his climactic reflex is automatically triggered. Again, this reduced reactivity occurs simply from the exposure of spending more time in the sexual experience.

However, the actual control men and women can exert sexually is exceedingly difficult to account for. The professional literature has not even attempted an explanation of it. Dr. Steven Levine, writing in the journal *Medical Aspects of Human Sexuality*, declared that the sexual self-control men learn develops "miraculously."

Women and men are unable to say exactly *how* they consciously increase or decrease their excitement, even though they *can* do it. It is an ability that eventually everyone will develop or catch on to, by remaining in the sexual milieu. Hence the thrust of the treatment is simply to direct the couple to refrain from ending the sexual experience through accidental orgasm. If one just continues making love, eventually he will learn to exercise, for all practical purposes, control over his sexual excitement; but he won't be able to say how.

Most descriptions of how people control their sexual excitement involve vague, fleeting references to subtle internal cues. These cues vary from person to person, whether one is trying to lower sexual excitement or to increase the level of arousal, as when one is consciously trying to reach a climax. The inability to say exactly *how* one controls sexual excitement is strikingly reminiscent of people using biofeedback equipment to regulate body states ordinarily thought to be involuntary. Blood flow, for example, can largely be controlled by self-awareness. If a person knows the temperature of his or her fingers (with or without the help of a biofeedback machine), he or she can cause blood to flow to and from those fingers, raising and lowering their temperature. But they can't say precisely *how* they do it. They too speak of subtle cues, vague and ineffable.

Sexual excitement, of course, is much more complicated than venereal engorgement. It is a whole-body state, an emotion in itself. Nevertheless, by simply remaining in a sexual experience with an awareness of the level of sexual excitement, one finds sooner or later than he or she can enhance or diminish that excitement.

The inability to say *how* reveals that control is not entirely voluntary. Lovers find that their control may vary somewhat, even from experience to experience. One time it may seem like, in Noyes's words, "confining oneself to the areas of easy rowing"; another time it may seem, in the words of the Taoist text, like "riding a galloping horse with rotten reins." But the variety in self-control is not something to lament; it adds a spice to one's sex life in a way that perfect control every time could not.

Although delightful at first, hitting a home run on every pitch, making a hole-in-one on every golf swing, picking every number that comes up on a roulette wheel would eventually become an utter bore. So, too, although self-control is an initial relief to those who have none, perfect voluntary control of every experience would make sex a bit plastic, almost as surely as coming too fast every time is no fun at all. The surprise that comes from a mixture of discipline and spontaneity is an essential ingredient in all human endeavor. Even after one has learned to voluntarily control one's sexual excitement, he will, thankfully, have to stop and calm down from time to time, and sometimes he will find that he has waited too long to stop. His control is not always entirely perfect, not black and white, not true or false, not scientific: It is an art.

Perhaps the fact that one cannot simply voluntarily raise and lower one's excitement, but that it does happen spontaneously, points to the mystical explanation that coitus reservatus is the most natural way to make love, and will naturally occur unless one pushes oneself into a pattern of forced, hurried orgasms. This also explains why the procedure, the how-to of learning to experience extended lovemaking, is primarily a set of instructions to stop deliberately doing that which brings about an orgasmic response, allowing coitus reservatus to occur naturally.

Perhaps the vision that coitus reservatus occurs spontaneously, while orgasm is the result of voluntary, deliberate effort, also explains why Shere Hite's interviews revealed that women who reached orgasm most easily during intercourse essentially did it themselves, by adjusting their positions, movements, or timing, while those who had trouble tended to expect their partners to "give" them orgasms or for it to happen without effort.

The real question, then, is not, "How does coitus reservatus work?" but, "Why would anyone make love in a way that prevents sex from being a timelessly endless expression of intimate love?"

3

Mystical Sex as Meditation

Jesus speaks of taking no thought for the morrow, "no thought" being the literal equivalent of *wu-nien* in Zen Buddhism, and of what I have called mystical silence, in which one is simply aware of what *is* in the here and now, without verbal or ideational comment.

In My Own Way
ALAN WATTS

TO ATTAIN MYSTICAL EXPERIENCE DURING LOVEMAKING, the mystical literature recommended that one fix, hold, stop, interrupt, contain, or stabilize thought. Mysticism asserted that one should approach sex with an empty mind, a void mind, no mind, original mind, even mindlessness. This instruction, "interrupt your thoughts," has been wildly misinterpreted. It has often, very wrongly, been taken literally to mean that mystics shun all mental activity and feature instead a blank, unaware, unconscious, numb, nonfunctioning state of mind, one which has closed out the world and locked away life.

What is really being recommended is that one stop a particular *type* of thinking: the verbal, judgmental, conceptual, theoretical, labeling, evaluative, representational, linear, running-internal-commentary-to-oneself type of thinking. This is thinking in which one's every experience, perception, or sensation is subvocally stated in words, given a positive or negative philosophical valence, explained to oneself according to some theory, affixed with a name, and linked with other conceptions by an abstract system of verbal rules of language called logic.

This mode of thought is associated with the left hemisphere of the human brain and generally takes the form of a subvocal monologue or dialogue. It is only this sort of thinking that mysticism rejects, or at least suggests that one minimize to allow a left and right hemisphere balance.

At the same time that one stops verbal thinking in mystical sex, one is completely aware of what's going on. In the spirit of "drinking from the fountain of life," mysticism recommends that one fully, totally, directly experience and participate actively and creatively in sex. One is completely awake, aware, involved, and absorbed—but without describing every part of the experience to oneself in words as it's going on. In mystical sex, lovers are *more* mentally aware, able to concentrate and get into it, by virtue of the fact that they are not thinking, because the direct perception of whatever is happening is not being filtered through a screen of internal soliloquy.

All higher integration—creative genius itself, whether scientific, artistic, or nurturing—involves the ability to contain or hold in one's mind the multidimensional aspects of any issue, rather than to consider them linearly, piecemeal, one at a time. As in all meditation, mystical sex favors the creative, perceptive, intuitive, feeling of experiencing directly. Without describing every sensation to oneself, without thinking, "Oh, that's good!" one just feels the physical sensations that occur. In mystical sex, a man and a woman are open to sensation, feeling it but not evaluating it, experiencing it fully but not listing what they're experiencing. Evaluative thought is contained, and the mind is allowed to grasp automatically, effortlessly, all at once whatever perceptions are occurring.

Meditation and Sex

When I say that mystical sex is a form of yoga or meditating during sex, on sex, or within the context of sexual love, I mean something quite specific: that it includes both a total mental absorption in the direct experience of sex, and an active, creative involvement in lovemaking—but not thinking. Making love without running internal commentary about the experience or anything else is precisely what was meant when the mystical traditions said that lovers should contain thought.

In this respect, the meditative mental approach to mystical sex is no different from the approach to any properly understood and carried out yoga or meditation. In fact, one can (and often probably should) apply this approach to just about any activity—eating, sleeping, breathing, carpentry, archery, tent-making, motorcycle maintenance, cooking a small fish, governing a great state, serving tea, making love. Done properly, almost anything can lead eventually to mystical experience. And, at the same time, this meditative attitude leads to much better results or performance. This is what baseball great Yogi Berra was referring to when he said, "You can't think and hit at the same time." (It wasn't that this Yogi's I.Q. wasn't high enough.)

To be sure, verbal thinking is very useful in its place, such as in giving instructions, making plans, or for entertainment. We all make covert verbal comments to ourselves to some extent. Some of us do it relatively seldom, while others are walking word processors who can't enter a room without registering every detail: "There's a pretty purple chair. . . . That picture's not hung straight. . . . What should I do now? . . . That plant needs watering. . . . Where is everyone? . . . Look at all those books. . . . I like this table. . . . It's oak." Many people can't sit still without doing some kind of verbal computation.

There is a broad spectrum of a "normal" in the amount of verbal thinking. But it is crucial in mystical sex that this is minimized at least to the extent that it doesn't interfere with or inhibit emotional intimacy and the achievement of mystical experience.

On the other hand, verbal communication and language itself can be approached from the no-thought state of mind. All speaking, listening, reading, writing, and even subvocal self-talk *can* be spontaneous, unfettered, and problem-free. The system of intellectual or jhana yoga, a cognitive meditation from which the word Zen was originally derived, is a way of using language spontaneously, naturally, being purposelessly absorbed in it. For example, when listening to someone talking, our minds understand perfectly well if we simply hear the sensation of the voice as a noise or sound. In fact, we understand someone speaking to us *more* clearly if we don't make some sort of verbal paraphrase to ourselves after each sentence.

In reading, the same principle applies—you don't have to translate or even say printed words to yourself; just allow yourself to see them. This is the theory behind speed reading, which is much faster and promotes better comprehension than reading subvocally. The point is that *anything* can be approached from a no-thought point of view.

Even silly things can be approached with *reservatus mentis*. Students of yoga and meditation frequently concentrate on their navels or magic sounds or supposedly secret phrases or weird body postures of some kind. This can have a terrific calming, relaxing effect and help to clear one's mind, and it's a good exercise for tense, highly stressed people and those with runaway left-brain activity. But let's face it, chanting is relatively boring, especially compared to making love. What isn't? That's the beauty part! Mystical sex was widely regarded as the fastest, easiest, and most natural practice through which one could attain mystical experience.

Actually, as Alan Watts revealed in his *Psychotherapy East and West*, when properly understood and carried out, yoga is roughly equivalent to our concept of psychotherapy. We will see shortly how most of the mental techniques of sex therapy are basically yoga principles applied to sex.

However, when we speak of techniques for the attainment of yogic or therapeutic goals as the result of certain procedures (coitus reservatus, containing thought, or any other), we can miss the deeper point, as Watts described it:

> Sexual yoga needs to be freed from a misunderstanding attached to all forms of yoga, of spiritual "practice" or "exercise," since these ill-chosen words suggest that yoga is a method for the progressive achievement of certain results—and this is exactly what it is not.

That is to say, the mystical experience comes about by the total spontaneous absorption, awareness, and concentration in each immediate sensational moment of the present here-and-now of sexual activity, without any thoughts of future goals or purposes, including sexual adequacy or the experience of transcendental consciousness.

The mystical traditions are quite clear when they talk about stabilizing thought. And they express this approach in many different ways. As Henri Maspéro pointed out, for the Taoists, the heart, rather than the brain, was the organ of wisdom and spirit. The brain was the organ of language, theory, and belief—a useful but inferior role. Of course, they knew then, as we know today, that this distinction in function holds true not for the brain and heart, but for the two modes of thought.

The primary characteristic of Tantrism, according to Eliade, is its "anti-ascetic, anti-speculative attitude," full involvement of the senses, without musing *about* what one is sensing. Tantra has been called "that which brings emancipation from the bondage of *maya*." *Maya* is the spell or illusion of words, language, concepts, and verbal theories; in general, it is a confusion between reality and its description, the territory and the map, the meal and the menu. The menu has its place, but it is not very nutritious. The illusion of *maya*, reification, believing that one's abstract thoughts have a tangible reality of their own, is what gives such power to words and allows popular religions and ideologies to hold such sway over the masses.

In making love, when one stops thinking, in the mystical sense, something very interesting occurs: One is able to concentrate completely on the immediate present moment and all that is occurring, while the hang-ups of the past and the goals and purposes strived for in the future no longer enter into and interfere with lovemaking. Being mentally absorbed, lovers feel what is actually happening, a union—a real, not a symbolic, communion.

In order to stop thinking, one may want to be aware of his or her current pattern of thought during lovemaking. We can start by identifying several patterns of self-talk during sex, including examples of psychopathic sexuality, sexual dysfunction, and "healthy" sex.

Styles of Thought during Sex

Men and women who experience mystical sex are quite aware that they stop thinking. They abandon verbal thinking and allow themselves to be carried away by the feelings and sensations of lovemaking.

On the other hand, many people who don't experience mystical sex are often unaware or unclear about their accompanying mental activity. There are many patterns or styles of thought that can interfere with mystical sex. One's mental activity during sex may follow a consistent pattern, or it may change according to one's mood or partner. It may be barely conscious, or it may be so dominant that it keeps a couple from making love altogether. Thought patterns may occur with a sex life that is healthy, ho-hum, dysfunctional, psychiatrically disturbed, or so sparse, so infrequent, that couples have forgotten what it's like.

We can learn a lot about ourselves when we make love. Particularly during unhurried sex that lasts indefinitely, one can examine the thoughts and images that come to mind during lovemaking—or before, or after, for that matter. On the one hand, an image or even a flood of thoughts and feelings can be unleashed during sex, in the form of fantasies, fears, memories, roles, and a running, inner commentary of all sorts. These may originate from various sources—the ego, the conscience, or the unconscious, collective and personal. On the other hand, one's conceptions about sex may be only vague images of how sex ought to proceed.

One may find that his or her thoughts during sex will require a deeper reflection and an insightful, even professional examination. Or perhaps it's all very obvious and has been for a long time. Or, one may want to jot some notes after keeping an eye on one's mental activity.

To be sure, such self-awareness is just the kind of thing the mystical literature suggests getting away from. But this examination would be a step en route to eliminating that self-conscious self-talk that interferes with mystical experience. Couples usually find that it's really not that difficult to get in touch with this aspect of their lovemaking.

When the mind wanders during sex, thoughts may be random or specific, they may or may not be related to sex, and they may be recurrent or unpredictable. The purpose these thoughts serve may not be obvious. Constant self-talk may or may not be typical of a person's general stream of mental activity. This is equally a problem for men and women; many of either sex at first cannot stop a verbal routine from coming to mind, streaming through the conscious awareness, and inevitably preventing a real mental involvement in the act of making love.

Certain common styles or patterns of sexual expression tend to be associated with characteristic types of mental content. Let us describe a few of these.

Pathological Self-Talk

First, there is a type of mental thought associated with a quasi-pathological condition acted out or, more specifically, internally crystallized during sex. This could reflect, for example, a disturbed attitude toward sex, or intimacy, or one's own body, or toward self-control, emotional or physical, or toward the opposite sex, as with this excerpt from Henry Miller's novel, *Tropic of Cancer*:

'I try all sorts of things,' he explains to me. 'I even count sometimes, or begin to think of a problem in philosophy, but it doesn't work. It's like I'm two people, and one of them is watching me. I get so goddamned mad at myself that I could kill myself, and in a way that's what I do every time I have an orgasm. For one second like I obliterate myself. There's not even one me then, there's nothing, not even a cunt. It's like receiving communion. Honest, I mean that. For a few seconds afterwards I have a fine spiritual glow, and maybe it would continue that way indefinitely—how can you tell?—if it weren't for the fact that there's a woman beside you and then the douche bag and the water running, all those little details that make you desperately self-conscious, desperately lonely. And for that one moment of freedom you have to listen to that love crap. It drives me nuts sometimes. I want to kick them out immediately. I do that now and then. But that doesn't keep them away. They like it in fact. The less you notice them the more they chase after you. There's something perverse about women. They're all masochists at heart.'

'But what do you want of a woman, then?' I demanded.

Although not necessarily delusional, per se, this example reveals an unconscious sadistic attitude toward women, a fear of love, and a lack of capacity for intimacy during or after sex. The character is so wrapped up in his own mental scenario, purposefully and successfully thinking to himself, and generally so self-absorbed that he becomes "two people"—one spectating, one performing, both complaining that the woman is making him self-conscious, making him think while making love.

This is a good example of how one's thoughts during sex can affect one's performance and experience of lovemaking. Perhaps this disturbed individual could find some salvation in mystical sex—that is, in *not* thinking, whether about philosophy, counting, himself, or anything else imaginary, but instead in perceiving the reality of the intimacy with his partner. Perhaps instead of his brief, momentary feeling that "it's like receiving communion," he could experience that feeling without end during spontaneous, meditative coitus reservatus.

Incidentally, the late eighteenth-century writings of the prolific Marquis de Sade described just about every possible sexually perverse behavior in details that neither the *Psychopathia Sexualis* of Krafft-Ebing nor the *Diagnostical and Statistics Manual* of the American Psychiatric Association could possibly match, try as they might. Sadism, named for him, was only one of the many categories of weird acts he extolled. Yet he virtually never gave us a glimpse of the inner mental activity, the cognitive subvocal workings of his many characters. Instead he reduced the depth and flavor of his stories to the banal drone of modern medical texts, once the initial shock at his incredibly grotesque vulgarity wears off.

Part of Henry Miller's excerpt above, "I even count sometimes, or begin to think of a problem in philosophy," reminds us of the attempt on the part of many men to control their sexual excitement and avoid premature ejaculation by following the old wives' (and old doctors') formula: "Think of other things." Their thoughts during sex could be of a problem in philosophy, the stock market, a mathematics table, a sports event, a frightening experience, or an unhygienic or degrading scene.

Some years ago, spoofing this strategy in one of his stand-up comedy routines, Woody Allen gave this story:

It's two o'clock in the morning, and I get my date back, and the two of us are alone, and we're going pretty good.

I have to explain this very delicately because it's very tentative:

As I am an inordinately passionate man— volatile, sensual, in general, a stud. In order to prolong the moment of ecstasy . . . I think about baseball players. All right, now you know.

The two of us are making love violently, and she's digging it, and I figure I better start thinking of baseball players quickly. So I figure it's one out in the ninth and the Giants are up.

Mays lines a single to right. He takes second on a wild pitch.

Now she's digging her nails into my neck. I decide to pinch-hit for McCovey. Alou pops out. Holland singles. Mays holds third. Now I got a first and third situation, two outs, the Giants are behind one run. I don't know whether to squeeze or steal. . . .

She's been in the shower for ten minutes already. . . .

I can't tell you any more, it's too personal. . . .

OK: The Giants won!

To say the least, thinking of other things really isn't a very serviceable way to make love, to control sexual excitement, or to enter into mystical experience. Instead, as we saw in chapter 2, complete awareness and involvement while not thinking is the ideal state of mental activity for learning to make love as long as both partners want. The direct, full experience of one's sexual excitement, without distracting inner commentary, not only allows one to know automatically when to stop or slow down so that orgasm doesn't interrupt the experience, but provides the immediate feedback of sensation that is the key to being able spontaneously to raise and lower one's excitement. Thinking of other things—that is, verbally thinking, period—is counter-productive to self-control, as well as being unromantic and generally no fun. Much more often, in fact, a running inner commentary causes rather than prevents a sexual dysfunction.

Dysfunctional Self-Talk

Another kind of mental content is associated with patterns of sexual dysfunction, especially some women's difficulty in achieving orgasm, and some men's difficulty in achieving or maintaining an erection. These sexual dysfunctions can occur on a couple's first sexual encounter, or as a result of a personal or interpersonal trauma, or as a result of situational stress. They can be longstanding patterns, or they can evolve gradually over some time. For males or females, these sexual dysfunctions have in common a pattern of thought during sex. Sex therapists have long recognized the connection between various thoughts during sex and certain male and female sexual dysfunctions, so that there are a few almost predictable kinds of thoughts that create the emotions inhibitory of sexual excitement and functioning, such as guilt, fear, anxiety, and worry.

One could have a fear of being punished somehow for engaging in sex. This could be a picture of demons and hellfire, a memory of parents or clerics scolding. Or one could be worried about an actual danger, as when a couple engages in an illicit liaison, or one not protected from unwanted pregnancy or venereal disease.

Thoughts that lead to sexual anxiety and dysfunction could involve an inner commentary as to the adequacy of one's own sexuality. It could be self-doubt about one's physiology, one's body, or its response. Or it can be a fear that one doesn't know what to do, or can't do it well enough. Such spectating and commentary about one's own sexual performance sets up a classic self-fulfilling prophecy, in that the fear of failure and of subsequent rejection itself will be the cause of the actual, consequent failure.

Warren Farrell, a lecturer/author on men's and women's liberation, described this kind of thinking in his book, *Why Men Are the Way They Are*:

> By suggesting that a man's power is located in his penis, the word *impotence* reinforces a man's self-consciousness about his penis, thereby reinforcing a likely problem: self-consciousness. In my work with men's groups, I find approximately 90 percent of so-called "impotence" to be catalyzed by some combination of *self-consciousness and fear of rejection* or, on the other hand, simple *distraction*. When the catalyst occurs at a moment when we are expecting a body organ to change its shape, *the body organ cannot concentrate*. Our self-consciousness prevents loving consciousness.

And, of course, self-consciousness prevents a higher, mystical consciousness.

Distracting Self-Talk

A third category of thoughts that inhibit simple sexual functioning has to do with outside distractions. These are not only such thoughts as whether the kids will hear or walk in, whether one will get to work on time, who's calling on the telephone, or even occasionally, as the joke goes, whether or not the ceiling needs painting. There are also distracting thoughts about life in general, especially if there is a crisis or any other circumstance that is taking precedence over sex. Loss of a job or a loved one, an illness, or any other problem or source of stress or depression can distract from not thinking. I have had many male and female clients who understand why they lose their appetite, sleep, and concentration under stress, but are shocked at their inability to function sexually. Concern about life-style or nonsexual problems doesn't have to be a crisis. It can develop over years, often quite accidentally and unconsciously.

Another broad category of thoughts associated with sexual dysfunction is focused on the overall relationship of the couple. Many men, but perhaps even more women, find themselves distracted during sex by issues in the relationship. In fact, as was shown in Seymore Fisher's extensive survey, *Female Orgasm*, no factor is more important to a woman's orgasmic responsiveness than a good relationship with her partner. But this is by no means an exclusively female issue; both women and men can become understandably perplexed when their partners want to make love after a bitter disagreement. I don't recommend that couples make love in the middle of an argument. My advice is to work things out in words first: That's a useful application of verbal thought, whether it takes a half hour of sensitive discussion or embarking on several months or years of intensive marital therapy.

It is typically a combination of such thoughts during sex that will constitute or even force a running commentary, and foster confusion, anxiety, distraction, and sexual dysfunction for one or both partners.

Adequate Sexual Performance

Thought patterns also are typically associated with regular, so-called healthy sex. When sex is satisfactory and even good and takes place regularly, men and women still tend to have a picture of how sex should go, how it should progress from beginning to end. It is this preconception of how sex *should* proceed that forms the content of their mental activity while making love. A little of this and that, foreplay-wise . . . then a certain amount of intercourse, with a clever position switch or two . . . all leading to orgasm (multiple, simultaneous, whatever you will) . . . each step brought on by one means or another—variety being the spice of life, as we know.

And there's nothing wrong with such a scenario, is there? But to the extent that a couple is following a plan or a set of guidelines, whether or not it is consciously clear, whether or not it's repetitious or innovative, whether or not the couple notices the pleasure along the way, to that extent the couple misses the here and now, and keeps mystical sex at arm's length. In other words, even if sex is adequate, lovers are often not really, totally involved in the immediate present, but instead are proceeding ahead toward a future endpoint. They may reach that point and be happy with it, but it brings them up far short of mystical experience.

One need not follow a plan, script, or picture of cagy or cool, effective, or ever so tastefully kinky sexual moves and things to do in bed. Things go best if one does nothing at all, but lets his or her body move spontaneously, of its own accord.

I am not against variety, in sex or anything else. But variety can be either natural or artificial, spontaneous or forced, real or phony. It is only through letting one's body do what it wants that sex is innovative, creative, surprising, renewed. Fake sexual variety derives from reading or hearing or thinking about "new" sex acts, positions, settings, zones, and techniques, and carrying out a performance accordingly. Whether in holding hands, oral sex, a back rub, or fancy fucking, the point is *not* to mentally review the right steps while faithfully executing them. We'll do much better without a sexual script.

One can be a perfectly boring lover, a real dud, despite

clearly performing some version of Masters and Johnson's glorified four stages of adequate sexual response and thus qualifying himself as normal or, more technically, "non-dysfunctional." The problem is that when one tries to follow a picture of how sex should proceed, no matter how flexible or innovative this scenario is, sex will eventually become tiresome, degenerating into a search for novelty.

The search for novelty in sex predictably leads not only to a never-ending and self-defeating hunt for newer, sexier, wilder, more erotic things to try, but to new partners as well. When sex has a map, script, or any goal or purpose, it becomes predictable, even if the goals are being achieved. Many sexual relationships begin adequately, even quite erotically, only to fizzle out with time. For many couples, initial sexual experiences are their most exciting because the unique newness of the encounter, the never-before experienced other body, and all the new physical sensations and reactions consume their thoughts and attention, allowing them to be mentally absorbed in each present moment of the encounter, and to function accordingly well. As the novelty wears off and predictability sets in, the minds wander; various distracting and inhibiting thoughts creep back in, interfering with the total involvement in the here and now, and trivializing the experience. Functional couples begin to experience an unemotional sex life.

In many of these cases, normal, sexually responsive men and women who know each other's bodies and know exactly, efficiently how to produce orgasms in the other, will accordingly become excited, go through their sexual routine, reach climaxes—and yet be miles away from the experience and each other, a sort of masturbation à deux, at best. At worst, making love with a stream of internal commentary can be unpleasant, distasteful, and uncomfortable. Eventually one partner grits his or her teeth and wishes or even openly encourages the other to "hurry up and get it over with." Then it becomes easier for one partner or both to stop having sex entirely, although it may happen quite unconsciously, and may even be rather confusing.

This change is chalked up to an assumption that the thrill always goes out of relationships after a while. But this is not necessarily true. A couple does not have to lose loving, sexual feelings and chemistry, and those feelings can be regained if they are lost. In many cases, they can be generated even if they were never there in the first place.

The reasons couples lose their sexual feelings is not time or familiarity, any more than contempt or any other emotion is necessarily fostered through those factors. When an otherwise happy couple has lost the sexual component of their otherwise healthy relationship, there is a concrete, identifiable problem: thinking during sex and, frequently, imagining that there is a right, adequate, or healthy way in which sex should proceed. That very picture, whatever it may be, is an example of the kind of thoughts that the mystical traditions recommend one contain in order to bring about a mystical union and an altered state of consciousness.

Such a conceptual vision of how normal sex should proceed may be as grossly imagined as a pornographic movie, but more often is very subtle, even subliminal or unconscious. We saw in chapter 2 how St. Augustine, Freud, Kinsey, and Masters and Johnson all (for different reasons) pictured orgasm as the ultimate purpose of sexual response, as well as its greatest pleasure; whereas, in mystical sex, the goal is an altered state of consciousness, brought about by unhurried and open-ended intimacy with one's lover, for which any real or imagined endpoint is inhibitory.

Table 2 shows a few of the countless possible sex plans that govern and control lovers' sex lives. They are arranged according to the purpose one may be striving to accomplish in sex, a psychological motivation behind each purpose, and the audience for whom one's sexual script is acted.

Table 2

Conceptions about Sex That Preprogram Lovemaking

Purpose of Sex	Motivation	Sex Plan	Audience
To be a "good" lover	Pride	Technical performance of sex variety and novelty	One's own ego
To avoid sin	Guilt	Neurotic celibacy or abstinence	One's own conscience
To relieve tension	Anxiety	Forced masturbation to orgasm, whether using hand or partner	One's own body
To get it over with	Duty	Submit until partner's orgasm	The ceiling
To maintain status quo	Equilibrium, habit	Do what one has always done	The relationship
To be normal	Shame	Keep pace with published trends	Sociologist/psychiatrist
To avoid intimacy	Schizoid fear	Brief promiscuous affairs	Strangers
To conceive children	Survival of species	Fertilization	The gametes
To enjoy sex, intimacy, pleasure	Affection, love	Making love	Spouse, partner, lover, friend
An altered state of consciousness	Love, unity	None	The cosmos

Containing Thoughts during Lovemaking

Some men and women have no trouble whatsoever interrupting their thoughts during lovemaking. They can abandon themselves to pleasure and intimacy, experiencing them directly and fully without inner monologue. For others, this approach is so new that it doesn't even sound realistic, much less possible. Fortunately, it is not that difficult. What follows is a suggestion for controlling mental activity during sex so that it does not interfere with the attainment of mystical experience.

There is a fairly clear precedent for controlling left-brain thought common to all meditation and yoga systems, as well as to many modern psychotherapies, including sex therapy. Applied to sex, the major thrust of this process has to do with fixing and holding one's conscious attention and concentration on what is actually happening in each immediate present moment of lovemaking, that is, on the direct perception of sexual sensations and feelings as they occur.

As Maspéro stated in his *Taoism*:

> The expression *Cunsi* which I translated as "ecstatic meditation" means if one takes the sense of each of the two words separately "To hold one's thought firmly attached to . . ." "to apply one's thoughts to." Therefore we have the Taoist definition from the expression: "During *Cunsi* close your eyes and interrupt your thoughts."

As one begins to hold his or her attention firmly attached to the direct sensation of what is going on during sex, eventually one is able to experience his or her thoughts and evaluations as sensations themselves. One can then freely perceive these thoughts as they occur, and allow them to pass through one's mind. The important thing is that one does not get hung up on

113

his thoughts, identifying with his verbal, left-brain commentary and concentrating his attention on that self-talk. As one begins to focus on the direct sensory perceptions of lovemaking, it becomes evident that "those thoughts are occurring to me," rather than "those thoughts *are* me." Consequently, one can allow those thoughts to pass on through and out of one's awareness.

It isn't necessary to contain all thoughts whatsoever, totally or fanatically. They should be contained only enough so that they don't inhibit the experience of closeness and intimacy. That is, one need not entirely eliminate all left hemisphere activity in order to promote mystical experience, but rather bring the left and right brain functions into a harmony, balance, or integration. Some will have to minimize their thoughts during sex a little, some a lot; others already experience lovemaking with stabilized thought.

Thought Stopping

One of behavior therapy's oldest techniques was actually called thought control or thought stopping, and was first used in the 1920s in the treatment of obsessions—persistent, uncontrollable thoughts, usually about one recurrent topic or mental scene. Thought stopping became a popular weapon in the behavior therapist's arsenal by the 1970s, and was used as an active, direct treatment of obsessional thinking, in contrast to the psychoanalytic method, which was slower, more indirect, but perhaps more comprehensive. Unfortunately, neither approach was very effective, and obsessive disorders remain particularly resilient against any kind of psychotherapy. However, the notion that one could direct one's attention and perception and thereby exert some control over one's cognitive function was eventually applied to the modification of sexual behavior, where it was found to be *very* helpful, especially, of course, when a sexual dysfunction was caused by a pattern of thought during love-making.

Today, meditation and thought stopping provide dramatic results in the treatments of such psychologically based symptoms as hypertension and depression. Most doctors still treat these symptoms with drugs; sexual symptoms were also treated mainly by drugs until the rise of the yoga-meditation techniques of sex therapy.

Sensual Concentration

Beginning in 1970, Masters and Johnson popularized the technique they called sensate focus, which is simply focusing one's attention on the sensations of lovemaking without letting one's mind wander. This technique, applied during a foreplay/massage exercise, was their first step in the treatment of every male and female sexual dysfunction. Kaplan referred to sensate focus as an "ingenious and valuable tool." In her *New Sex Therapy*, she wrote of how she would describe the exercise to her patients:

> I'd like you both to get ready for bed—to take your
> clothes off, shower, and relax. I want you (the
> woman) to lie on your belly. Then you (the man)
> caress her back as gently and sensitively as you
> can. . . . Concentrate only on how it feels to touch her
> body and her skin. In the meantime, I want you (the
> woman) to focus your attention on the sensations you
> feel when he caresses you. Try not to let your mind
> wander. Don't think about anything else, don't worry
> about whether he's getting tired, or whether he is en-
> joying it—or anything; let yourself feel everything.

Then, as was the psychiatric fashion of the day, Dr. Kaplan felt obliged to proceed in steps: "if neither becomes tense or turns himself/herself off, or escapes into fantasy, the experiences are repeated with the inclusion of genital stimulation in the prescription. (We call this 'sensate focus II.')"

In fact, the method of learning to have a meditative attitude in lovemaking need not be approached in any sort of hierarchic stages. It doesn't matter what one does or concentrates on. Furthermore, this approach is best not viewed as an exercise, tool, or technique for the attainment of a future goal—sexual adequacy, mystical experience, or any other—but as a means to immerse oneself in the present of what one is doing and experiencing, and thereby to stop thinking.

There are a number of aspects of sexual love to which one may wish to firmly attach his or her attention, en route to letting go of thought and drifting away to the subtle plane of mystical consciousness. These aspects of sex may be active or passive; they may involve either touching or feeling or both at the same time. They can be general or specific, one feeling or several at once, or the sense of being one with your lover and the universe.

One may wish to start, for example, where sexual therapy ends, by concentrating on what your partner's body feels like as you touch it with your hand, caressing it gently, slowly, lovingly—or any other way you both like. Or, feel your partner's whole body with your whole body as you hold each other lovingly, maximizing body contact. As one concentrates on the direct perception of the sensations, it is not so difficult to realize and experience many sensations at once, throughout the body.

One can soon experience the sensations of active touching and receptive feeling at the same time, for each caress, each point of contact with your partner both gives and receives touch. You can feel what your lover's body feels like as you touch it, and you can perceive the sensations within your own hand or other parts of your body. One can shift one's attention back and forth between being feeler and toucher, or perceive the two at once—in fact, they are the same. You can begin to sense that active touching and receptive feeling are the same thing, differing only by a shift of attention. The way your lover's body feels is no different than the sensations in your hand as you touch it.

The important thing is that you experience the feelings directly, without having to say, "that's smooth," or "that's wet," or "that's firm," or at least not letting any commentary obscure and interfere with the sensations themselves. This concentration applies to each of the senses, not just touch. The sense of taste— that goes with the sense of touch, doesn't it! And what variety in one body!

The sense of smell—you can sense yourself, your partner, the two of you together. Sense your natural scents in addition to the perfume and cologne you're wearing, not to mention soap, shampoo, makeup, deodorant, and hair spray; the complex elements in your breaths; the scent of the room you're in, or of a warm breeze, or incense in the air. There is no limit to what you can create. These each cause a reaction, a sensation, an emotion that needs no further description.

And the sounds of each other, in breathing, gasping, rolling, and laughing, m-m-m-ing, licking one's lips or the other's lips. And the music of each other's voices, when there's something to be said, or whispered, or shouted, or screamed. You can hear the sounds that you make as well as those of your partner, and you can sense the inaudible vibration of your bodies rubbing together, as they begin to glow in harmony. You can let yourself be receptive to these sounds as pure sound, without need of interpretation or analysis or additional meaning. Hear them as noise or as music, allowing the sounds to fall upon your ears, without needing to say anything to yourself about it.

And the sense of sight, what delicate sensations the eye can perceive, even in darkness. The colors, the shapes and textures, bright or dim, and the subtle changes in appearance that can occur in, on, and throughout your partner's body and your own. As with hearing, let the images come to your eyes. Effortlessly allow yourself to see everything within your field of vision without identifying individual things and parts of things. Let your eyes focus where they want. See without looking, just by having your eyes open, the whole great kaleidoscopic mélange. Or look, stare, deeper, more closely, more focused. Then go back to no focus. The two visions are the same, differing only in a shift of attention, unless you shift your focus onto something else.

As you begin to fix your attention on individual sensations and feelings, without thinking about them, you will also begin to be able to perceive all the senses at once, coordinated naturally and effortlessly in a symphony of experience. You have always had this ability; it was only the conscious self-talk that interfered with your direct, simultaneous awareness of all your senses. With each of the senses, as with touch, a change in direction of attention leads to interpreting one's sensations as either subjective or objective. That's the way he looks, or that's the retinal sensation in my eyes. That's how she sounds, or those are my eardrums vibrating. That is my partner's perfume, or those are the olfactory sensations activated within me. At this point, in direct perception without accompanying verbal evaluation, pure subjectivity is pure objectivity.

Mystical Awareness

Next, one may wish to focus attention on what one feels like as a whole, both as active and receptive lover. This is something more than just awareness of the five senses all at once. As you make love with your partner, regardless of what form that love-making takes, you find that your body as a whole begins to respond, not only with physical excitement but with an overall emotional state of being. The direct perception of that overall state is not only clearer, but it is possible only when you don't tell yourself how it feels.

Alternately, you can sense your partner as a whole. Again, this is much more than the addition of all the visual, olfactory, aural, tactile, and taste reactions your partner produces in you. Your partner's excitement, feelings, actions, reactions, and especially his or her overall "presence" are inevitably communicated, just as you express your inner experience by your presence. On the one hand, you can't know exactly what your partner is feeling, what is going on internally for the other; but on the other hand, everything she or he does, every sense you get from your partner, conveys the nature and the intensity of the excitement he or she is feeling.

It is this overall feeling in and of your partner that you can begin to concentrate on, fix your attention on, in order to stabilize your thoughts. And what a great thing to concentrate on, to meditate on—your partner's feelings. You don't have to believe in ESP or telepathy to experience the direct perceptual communication of your feelings to each other, not in words, but in a state of honest, spontaneous, loving, sincere, physical relationship. Words can only trivialize this message.

Or you may find that you are automatically holding your attention on both yourself as a whole and your partner as a whole at the same time. You are fully aware of the simultaneous effect you have on each other in the immediate present moment, the effect your actions and reactions have on each other, and how you are such a large part of what the other is perceiving and experiencing, each having just as much influence on the other.

Next, you may want to focus your attention on the fact that through sex, you and your partner have actually become physically connected—literally one with each other. Just as feeling that your body as a whole is more than the sum of your five senses at once, this connection is more than just concentrating on the two of you at the same time.

Then comes a realization, a feeling when joined in sexual love, whether or not it is intercourse per se, that a man and woman become literally, physically joined with not only each other, but unified with what is "not me," that is, the rest of the universe. You are wholly absorbed in the present moment, carried along together without any worry of an end, without a preconceived goal toward which you progress. It is not difficult to realize, to feel that one is no longer a separate one, but a part of a larger whole.

This actual unity is not something one has to imagine or pretend. It is a literal fact, the reality of which one need only perceive honestly and directly. As we allow ourselves to experience the fact of such physical and emotional unity with another, we also find that our ego boundaries, which artificially separate us psychically from the rest of the universe, also break down and we begin to feel ourselves swept away, carried along by natural forces over which we have freely relinquished an unnecessary struggle. Forces not simply bigger than ourselves, but forces of which we are integrally, organically, naturally a part.

Above all, we realize that we are beginning to drift away into mystical experience. As we're carried along, the distinction between "I'm doing it" and "it's happening to me," between "you" and "me" is broken down as well, and we realize the purposeless, effortless, spontaneous nature of mystical sex. When a man and woman let go of commentary as they make love, they also let go of past and future, their hang-ups, goals and purposes, distinctions and differences. Without any pre-planned purpose in lovemaking, lovers let go of what they're "supposed to" do or accomplish, and they don't push themselves around. They can allow their bodies to move naturally, spontaneously. Spontaneity is the third characteristic of mystical sex.

4

Mystical Sex and Spontaneity

Both [Taoism and Tantrism] practice "watching over the breath," because . . . their attitude to breathing is one of the main keys to understanding their attitude to sexuality.

According to some accounts, perfect mastery of the breath is attained when its rhythm comes to a stop—without loss of life. This is obviously a literalistic caricature. . . . Actually, "watching over the breath" consists in letting the breath come and go as it wants, without forcing it or clutching at it.

Nature, Man and Woman
ALAN WATTS

WHEN GOD CREATED ADAM AND BREATHED LIFE INTO him, He wasn't giving Adam mouth-to-mouth resuscitation; He was demonstrating the double meaning of "breath," found not only in the ancient Hebrew language, but in Chinese, Sanskrit, and Greek as well. Specifically, all the classic cultures used the term "breath" to denote what has been translated as life force, soul, or sometimes the essence of something. However, a better, modern, Western interpretation of breath as it was used in the mystical literature would be ego, will power, or deliberate action.

Therefore, when the mystics recommended that one contain or stop breathing during sex, they were not referring to respiration at all. They were suggesting that couples make love spontaneously, allowing sex to happen naturally, letting it flow along effortlessly, in the same way that our breathing automatically goes on and on without end, without thought, without effort, and without our having to deliberately "do" anything at all.

The suggestion that one make love without doing anything doesn't mean just lying there, frozen, dumb, limp, impassive, or dispassionate; that would be a deliberate, active inhibition of natural sexual expression. Spontaneity means letting one's body do what it wants without directing it one way or the other, forcing it, or inhibiting it. Then it will act as never before. Or, better, it means that lovers let their bodies automatically respond to each other, just by a sense of feel, trusting that they will intuitively work together. Then they certainly will do the right things for each other, in a way that would be impossible if the lovers consciously try to do what they think they should do, according to some preconceived, prearranged sex plan.

In mystical sex, lovers need to make no effort, furious, furtive, conscious, or otherwise, to thrust, hump, pump, jump, bump and grind, rub, writhe, wriggle, wiggle, shimmy or shake, sock, knock, rock and roll. Swinging, swaying, pressing, pushing, plunging, pulling, wham, bam, slam, bang, tango, fandango, mambo, hula, boogaloo, cha-cha-cha! You don't have to think about those or any other motions if you let your natural, instinctive, inner knowledge take you along, a long way past such regular, basic fucking. Thank you, ma'am! Lifting, sinking, in-out, way out, way in, up-down, around-and-around, side-to-side, to sidesaddle, high-in-the-saddle, bareback, way back, backbone slip. "If I hold you any closer, we'll be in back of each other," quipped Groucho Marx. Back and forth, linear, circular, rotating, revolving, vibrating, figure eight, parabolic, peristaltic, gyroscopic, oceanic, or, as songwriter Warren Zevon put it, "like a Waring blender"—it's still regular pedestrian sex as long as one is carrying out, executing, or consciously performing such actions. It is the *effort* itself, the *willing*, the very *striving* to do it in such and such a way, just so, *on purpose*, that will prevent one from reaching the altered emotional plane of mystical experience.

This is why sex advice, whether ancient, modern, exotic, fancy, or enlightened, is bound to miss the point. Carrying out sex suggestions, in reality and by definition, prevents one from loving instinctively from the bottom of the heart, the small of the back, the pinnacle of the spirit. Spontaneous lovemaking will happen naturally *unless* you're following some sort of instructions, whether they're from Masters and Johnson, Xaviera Hollander, the *Kama Sutra*, the locker room, street, or barnyard, a classic novel, or a porno flick. No matter how grossly a pornographic movie displays "sex"—grossly as in both big and grotesque—it cannot even begin to show the most intimate, sensuous, sexy, *really* sexual aspects of lovemaking. Graceful ballroom dancing may paint a better picture; better yet is Latin dancing, which has been called "the vertical expression of a horizontal intention."

To experience mystical sex, putting forth any deliberate effort whatsoever is quite unnecessary. Because when two people are joined indefinitely and able to feel their connection and responses without inner commentary, lovers find that, just as easily as they breathe, their bodies will begin a sacred dance. They will be carried along in a flowing, effortless, swelling wave, an unending undulation in which their bodies do just the right things for each other, taking them past the threshold of ecstasy to the subtle plane of mystical experience.

Spontaneous sex is effortless, not only in genital or pelvic sex. All touching, kissing, hugging, caressing, holding, cuddling, snuggling, nuzzling, nibbling, kneading, squeezing, licking, tasting, stroking, sucking, drinking, inhaling, exhaling, blowing, teasing, cooing, humming, m-m-m-ing, all movement, touch, give and take, all feeling—all connection takes care of itself. Lovemaking is coordinated, immediate, sensuous, effortless; it happens automatically without lovers willfully having to do anything at all—it's a cakewalk!

This chapter will elaborate on what is meant by spontaneity in lovemaking, and give some suggestions as to how lovers can get in touch with their natural ability to realize sexual spontaneity. Let us look at how spontaneity has been grossly misinterpreted by the majority of serious commentators on mystical sex. Begin the beguine.

Confusion about "Not Breathing"

Spontaneity is a central theme in mysticism, philosophically as well as sexually. In the mystical literature spontaneity was sometimes presented by the suggestion that one stop, fix, retain, stabilize, arrest, hold, or contain one's breath.

Of the three aspects of mystical sex, the injunction to contain breathing is the most widely misunderstood by translators and commentators on the mystical literature. Many authors have taken the recipe "hold your breath" more or less literally, apparently under the impression that mystics were trying to absorb air without inhaling. Or they thought that oxygen deprivation had something to do with mysticism or mystical sex, or that somehow mystics had less need to respire, or that the arrest of breath promoted transcendence, or that in mystical experience there is no need to breathe. All of this is not only ridiculous, but is a perfect example of the claims to miracles and magic powers that are characteristic of popular theology and are emphatically rejected by mysticism.

For example, June Singer, Jungian analyst and author of two otherwise fine books on sexuality, *Androgeny* and *Energies of Love*, tried to state how the mystics' "not breathing" was involved with transcendental, mystical experience: "Because they have transcended their mundane mode of existence, there is, accordingly, a near immobilization of breathing. . . . The regression [to mystical experience] is enhanced by the arrest of breathing." This is typical of the sentimental, quasi-rational explanations proffered by many writers about mysticism. But this is not really an explanation at all. It is simply a misstatement based on a misunderstanding of what is really meant by contain breath, which is: Let all your actions be as natural as your breathing.

A more subtle and widespread mistake with regard to not breathing seen in many works on mysticism is the idea that some kind of rigorous breath exercise and subsequent breath control have something to do with mystical sex. Readers are told: Don't start panting . . . breathe slowly . . . from the diaphragm . . . through the nose . . . out the mouth . . . mutter "Om" . . . with such and such a ratio: inhale, retain, exhale . . . put some rhythm into it . . . and above all, practice, practice, practice!

We also find countless lengthy treatises on breathing styles, patterns, synchronisms, techniques, rhythms, regulations, phasings, disciplines, and analyses, all of which completely miss the point: that breathing is merely a good example, a good demonstration of the mystical dictum, "What is spontaneous is better than what is deliberate." If we simply relax and watch our own breathing, without inhibiting it or trying to influence it in one way or another, it continues naturally in just the right way. So, too, with sexuality, and all of life.

Techniques and advice on breathing have basically the same problem as does sex advice (and all preaching for that matter). That is, by following breath advice, one necessarily introduces deliberate action, precludes spontaneity, and interferes with letting it happen naturally, from the heart or, in this case, the lungs.

If we view life as a great river that carries mankind along whether we swim with or against the current, spontaneity means going with the unique inner current that springs from within each of us. We continue breathing even if we force, grasp, or inhibit it in some way; but it goes better when we let it happen naturally. The less action we take, the less we deliberately do, the better.

Just as important, when we understand that the best way to breathe or to make love is known intuitively within each of us, and that we will be guided naturally along the right path if we allow ourselves to be, then we begin to see the experts and advice givers in a new light. They are pretending to set down external, official guidelines, rules, and directions for behavior that will instinctively happen anyway, teaching people what they already know how to do. Their effort to impose an illusion of authority is a political endeavor, a method of mass behavior control, and a principal function of popular theology.

Related to these common mistakes about not breathing is a popular misconception about the mythical power of various syllables, sounds, and vibrations, sometimes known as mantras. Traditional mysticism was interested in the nature of musical sound, particularly because of the intimate relationship among arithmetic, geometric, and harmonic proportion, an interest also reflected in mystical architecture. (This is why Goethe called geometry "frozen music.") But the mystical interest in sound and harmony has also been widely misinterpreted. A belief in special sounds, words, or phrases that confer some sort of preferential results or power to whoever recites or chants them, is the kind of phony magic that the world's popular theologies boast of, and that the mystical traditions categorically denounce.

Such use of mantras has been frequently associated with breath exercise and the literal regulation of breathing. Even the ordinarily reliable S.B. Dasgupta, a leading authority on Indian philosophy and religion, wrote that the use of the sounds or syllables "does not mean the mere chanting or muttering of the Mantra; it is, as it is with the school of Mantra-yoga, a yogic process for controlling the vital wind [breath] with the help of the Mantra." But, since breath in this context has nothing special to do with respiration, so, alas, the use of words or sounds as a magic, whether simply by uttering them or in conjunction with inhaling or exhaling in a particular manner, is superstitious make-believe, and has contributed to the popular confusion about mysticism. Amen.

There are many good reasons for chanting, singing, humming, or whistling a mantra, a song, an aria, a nursery rhyme, a poem, a prayer, or jazzy nonsense sounds as in scat singing. One might want to do so for a calming, relaxing effect; as a form of joyous, exhilarating exuberance; for entertainment or fun; as a group activity; because you feel like it, or for any other reason or combination of reasons, or for no reason—sometimes it just starts coming out. And, there is a place for breath exercises, whether aerobic, diaphragmatic, hyper-, hypo-, or any other regime of ventilation. One may wish to engage in breath exercise for help in singing better, losing weight, reducing stress, achieving altered consciousness, strengthening one's cardiovascular capacity—I heartily recommend all kinds of exercise and physical fitness. But there is nothing special about sounds or breathing that promotes mystical sex or an altered state of mind.

Spontaneity in the Mystical Literature

Spontaneity is one of the basic concepts in both mystical sex and mystical philosophy. Whether in making a decision or making love, mysticism suggests that we act spontaneously, allowing our minds and bodies to do what they want and trusting that we will do the right things if we let ourselves act freely and creatively, guided by feeling and intuition, without trying to govern or push ourselves around.

The mystical writings recommend natural, spontaneous behavior in shorthand by saying, "Stop breathing." But in the more elaborate discourses, the literature refers to spontaneous action in other terms. For example, spontaneous behavior is purposeless, effortless, nonstriving, noninterfering, uninhibited, unblocked, detached, laissez-faire, nonego, selfless, nonwishing, not grasping, unhesitating, not pursuing, not role-playing, and unforced. Such terms, at first blush, may sound rather vague, passive, and even contradictory. But they have a common theme and relation to mystical sex.

Essentially, these terms for spontaneity are ways of referring to action that emanates from the right hemisphere of the brain. Spontaneous behavior is expressed from the intimate, unitive, feeling, instinctive, perceptive part of us.

The verbal thinking, conceptually labeling left hemisphere is verbal-analytic on the mental level. On the behavioral level, it follows directions, carries out plans, consciously controls according to instructions, strives for goals, deliberately acts or inhibits, and performs other so-called ego functions. This deliberate left-brain action and inhibition interferes with right-brain behavioral spontaneity.

The mystical literature's ways of expressing spontaneous action (*non*striving, *non*ego, *non*interfering, purpose*less*, self*less*, etc.) constitute a negation of those controlling, left-hemisphere functions that prevent or interfere with spontaneity. The mystical writings use negations because there is no positive action one can take in order to be spontaneous. We cannot deliberately strive to act naturally, because such deliberate effort is precisely what prevents spontaneity. But spontaneity will occur naturally and automatically if not interfered with. Therefore, its attainment does not involve doing anything, but is accomplished by stopping, containing, arresting, desisting from that which interferes with it.

For example, when the mystics spoke of being detached, they did not mean being uninvolved. Quite the contrary, the key to mystical experience is a total, complete involvement and immersion in whatever one does, mentally and behaviorally. The detachment that is recommended is detachment from the analytic, instruction-following, mission-oriented aspect of ourselves.

This is not an all-or-nothing, black-and-white suggestion that all left-brain activity is harmful to mystical experience. As with "not thinking," what is called for in "not breathing" is a balance or integration, so that one's rational, controlling, left hemisphere activity is limited to the extent that it no longer interferes with spontaneity and the attainment of mystical experience. To achieve this balance, some will have to "stop breathing" a little, some a lot, and some people already approach life spontaneously.

Spontaneity has been compared to coasting on a bicycle, which is, as we all know, principally a flowing with the movement and doing relatively little, except perhaps leaning a bit this way or that. Most of us remember that it was awkward to ride a bike at first; kids think they must do something other than just balance with the flow. But how easy it is to ride a bicycle once it's rolling! It's so easy that it's something we never forget how to do.

And, of course, sex is much more natural than bicycling. Because sex is so natural, lovemaking is in fact the easiest thing one can do spontaneously. It is in this spontaneous feeling of flowing that the two sides of our minds are in balance, a harmony in which lovers make a kind of beautifully musical cosmic vibration.

Spontaneous Creativity

Although sex may be the easiest, fastest, and most natural endeavor that can be approached from the creative, spontaneous side of the brain, it is not the only one. Just as we saw that one could do anything without thinking, so too we can engage in any activity spontaneously, "without breathing."

Certainly, all art emanates from the creative, intuitive aspect within us. That is why we cannot tell someone how to be an artist, although Betty Edwards's very important book, *Drawing on the Right Side of the Brain*, does enable readers to get in touch with their innate artistic ability.

As she demonstrates, drawing realistic portraits has very little to do with coordination, dexterity, or manual skill. One mainly learns to *see* the way artists see. After only a few lessons, in which students learn how to see from the intuitive, spontaneous side of the brain, Edwards teaches anyone whose handwriting is readable or printing legible to draw on an artist level. Once people can see what they actually are seeing, unclouded by left-brain preconceptions and self-talk, the drawing of it is relatively easy.

A perfect example of nonart produced from the analytic, rule-following side of the mind is "painting by numbers," in which one merely places various colors within predrawn boundaries according to the numbers found in those spaces. It is not coming from within at all, but just following externally imposed instructions. And the painter isn't "seeing" a scene to paint, he is only recognizing concepts (numbers, colors) and following directions.

If one can visually perceive the world as it actually is, one then knows exactly what to draw, without covertly saying anything to himself or herself in words. At the same time, the hand knows how to draw without any instructions in the form of internal self-talk from the artist's left brain, or external instructions such as predrawn shapes.

Spontaneity is also what makes the difference when cooking is more than just following a recipe accurately, when singing or playing music is more than simply hitting the notes precisely, when dancing is more than the mere execution of the steps in time. Eugene Herrigel's *Zen in the Art of Archery* is a classic description of how one elevates sport to art through mental absorption and spontaneous involvement. We could say that anything can be an art when engaged in with the right attitude.

Depending on one's approach, even normal, everyday activities can be made artful or ceremonial, even sacred. The so-called Japanese tea ceremony is not a special series of ritual gestures. It differs from the ordinary routine chore of brewing tea only by one's inner state of mind; it is one's spontaneous involvement that makes it special. This is why tradition dictates that for those too poor to afford tea, the ceremony can be adequately carried out using just hot water.

Even breathing can be approached "without breathing," without doing anything, just by watching one's breath come and go. It is a fascinating, instructive exercise to shift one's perspective slowly back and forth from "I'm breathing" to "It's breathing me," then to both perspectives at once, and finally to *just* feeling oneself breathe without any kind of labeling at all.

Even what are usually thought of as verbal, rule-following, left-brain activities can be approached spontaneously. Mere role-playing is elevated to the art of acting when one is totally, spontaneously immersed in one's role, when one "becomes" one's character—that is the basis of so-called method acting. Conversely, many people live their real lives by playing roles that society has assigned them, mechanically, dutifully, desperately doing only what someone else says they're supposed to do.

Such a purely verbal endeavor as putting words on paper becomes the art of literature when it flows spontaneously from within, inspired. Otherwise, it is contrived and forced. In Truman Capote's words about such work, "It's not writing, it's just typing."

Even doing nothing can be raised to the level of an art when approached spontaneously. Whether in a goofy yoga position, or gently rocking on the front porch, sitting quietly, doing nothing can be serene, even transcendental, if one is not trying to accomplish something or covertly talking to oneself. Otherwise, it's hard to sit still, much less enjoy oneself; that's why some people "can't relax." The millions of people who don't sleep well often have a similar problem. Either they can't stop talking to themselves, or they deliberately try to fall asleep, and the effort to do so keeps them awake.

Sexual Spontaneity

Finally, much more easily and naturally than can bicycling, drawing, cooking, singing, playing music, dancing, archery, brewing tea, acting, writing, breathing, or sleeping, sex can be a sacred art, if approached spontaneously.

As a contrast to mystical sex, the mystical writings made numerous references to profane sex. This did not mean dirty, illicit, or abnormal sex; nearly the reverse, profane sex was "normal," average, regular, Masters-and-Johnson four-stages-of-sexual-response sex. It can certainly feel good, but it brings lovers far short of mystical experience because in profane sex, lovemaking is not approached spontaneously from within, but is carried out according to a preconceived, predetermined scenario. It is the venereal equivalent of painting by numbers, or *Sex by Prescription* as modern-day iconoclastic psychiatrist Thomas Szasz called his insightful book.

The spiritual and practical problem with most sex advice is that following or practicing a list of sexual instructions is necessarily not spontaneous. It is contrived, forced and un-natural, and assumes that a person doesn't know what he or she is doing. We actually don't *know* cognitively what we're doing—but our bodies do instinctively know what to do and will act accordingly if allowed to.

That sex advice inhibits spontaneity was just as real a problem in the ancient sex manuals as it is in today's sex therapies. In the first centuries of the Christian era, there arose in all the major cultures a certain style of sexual literature, typified by the *Kama Sutra* in India, the *Perfumed Garden* in the Arab lands, and the *T'ung Hsuan Tzu* in China. These works were very similar to each other and were actually just regular, pedestrian sex advice for the householder of the kind we might find today in a magazine advisor column. Liberally dished out, they covered such topics as the anatomy of the sexual organs (including such esoteric zones as the G-spot), the range of sizes and combinations of the male and female sex organs, various positions for sexual intercourse, oral sex techniques, differences in sex drives, types of kissing, methods of pelvic thrusting, issues of courtship and romance, and advice on what kind of husband or wife is or is not likely to be faithful.

These are very interesting topics, and they are an impor-tant part of making love. Who could have anything against such a study? But these bits of advice have nothing in particular to do with mystical sex, which is concerned more with the elevation of one's state of mind that results from the unhurried, meditative employment of just about any kind of spontaneous love-making.

Related to this sort of ancient sex advice was an erotic art, which has also been erroneously connected to the sexuality of the mystical traditions. In India, for example, as N.N. Bhattacharyya clarifies in his *History of the Tantric Religion*:

> From c. A.D. 900 onward, there was really an outburst of erotic expression—bold, frank, and gross, with countless varieties of copulative acrobatics—on the exterior and interiors of religious buildings. . . . But these are imaginative techniques having nothing to do with Hathayoga proper . . . not associated with Yogic techniques or aims. . . . The inspiration behind all these depictions is the Kamashastra literature meant for the titillation and pleasure of the aristocratic class and the wealthy city dwellers.

A similar confusion often arose with regard to Greek and Chinese erotic art, and has led to the numerous illustrations in today's popular books on Taoism and Tantrism. These are pictures of different sex acts and positions, sometimes beautifully depicted by stick figures, in woodblock prints, color paintings, on walls and vases, and through magnificent sculpture of all sizes and sorts. But, in fact, these positions have nothing in particular to do with mystical sex and the transportation of consciousness.

Whether it is artistically precise or vaguely imaginary, many people who function well enough sexually still consciously or unconsciously have a mental picture of what they ought to be doing sexually or of what moves they're supposed to make. They put themselves through certain paces and poses, consciously pushing themselves and their bodies around from this preconceived image of what's supposed to go on, and thereby forfeiting real spontaneity.

The How-to of Sexual Spontaneity

Instructions for spontaneity cannot be spelled out, because one cannot be spontaneous when following instructions.

Just as learning to draw spontaneously is not a question of improving manual dexterity, or coordination, or hand skill, but a matter of seeing the way an artist sees, to an even greater degree, spontaneity in lovemaking is not a more difficult discipline than having "regular" sex. It is not a skill one needs to practice. It is something innate that anyone can allow to happen.

In the same way that artistic spontaneity is a matter of *seeing* things as they actually are, spontaneity in lovemaking is principally a question of *feeling.* The direct experience of one's lover, the very feelings, the perceptual sensations will provide one the immediate, intuitive knowing, the psychological guide to what to do. Lovers respond effortlessly and naturally as one being. This is a major reason why mysticism placed such a premium on not thinking, on direct perception without conceptual, self-talk thought.

What follows are a few suggestions for getting in touch with one's natural, flowing, spontaneous response to one's feelings. They are not rules or techniques, but a sort of first push in the right direction for those who may want one, just as we may have needed a first push to get rolling when we learned to ride a bicycle. After that, it's so easy and naturally self-reinforcing that suggestions and instructions are pale and trivial in the face of the limitless creative capacity—in the poet Lord Byron's words, the "ten thousand delicate inventions"—which flows from within us once we get rolling.

Let us look now at three popular aspects or venues of lovemaking—kissing, touching, and the act—and see how to stop breathing, to stop doing that which interferes with spontaneity.

Kissing

A couple may want to get rolling by simply touching the tips of their tongues together, and doing nothing else except to feel and watch. Just be aware of the perceptions and sensations, one's own reaction to the other, the impulse to do. Just touch without directing one's tongue up and down, around and around, or in any other motion or deliberate action, and, just as important, without inhibiting it or holding it still.

In other words, simply let the tongue move as it wants to, feeling, tasting, even licking, flicking, rolling, turning, twisting, entwining, exploring, pushing away, drawing in, or none of that, just relaxed and feeling. Just let it happen—not you doing it, your tongue doing it, or your tongue not doing it.

Quickly you find that your tongue has, as they say, a mind of its own and knows exactly what to do. All you need to do is feel what your tongue actually feels. Directly, honestly experience whatever you are actually feeling and sensing. Sense not only the taste, but the warmth, wetness, and textures of the skin and breath. Experience everything, including all the changes occurring in yourself and your partner, from moment to moment, in response to each other's tongue tips.

Whether you spend a few moments or a few hours, you may want to taste and feel not only your lover's tongue, but lips, mouth, and any and every other part of your partner's body, according to interpersonal taste. There is no need to inhibit your lips and whole mouth from joining your tongue in joining your lover. How better than by such a sacred intimacy to know each other so directly and personally.

We could say that all oral sex is a kind of kissing and vice versa. One need not perform a certain series of acts or movements, but only allow one's mouth to do what it wants, to do whatever comes naturally, by a sense of intuitive feeling. This is why now-do-this, now-do-that oral sex instructions, whether found in the original, gilt-edged *Kama Sutra* or in the latest, hottest, biggest hardcover sex text, are nothing short of absurd.

In giving cunnilingus advice, one comedian suggested that men "lick the alphabet, especially capital T." But such deliberate calligraphy quickly degenerates into a series of disaffected jabs, stabs, slashes, wags, laps, slaps, slurps, and drooling, especially when compared with the four-dimensional, full-color stellar mandala of feeling that is set off within each other when a couple's kissing is allowed to happen by itself and flow along without end, as it wants to.

Touching

The same principle, naturally, holds not only for touching with one's mouth, but with one's hands as well. We can say that a loving, spontaneous caress is a divine kissing with one's hand.

Just as surely as there is something special about the touch and feel of one's lips, mouth, and tongue, so too there can be something extraordinary about the touch of one's hands. As Honoré de Balzac recounted in *The Physiology of Marriage*:

> The hand is the medium through which the whole of man's power is made manifest, and it is worthy of remark that men of powerful intellect nearly always have beautiful hands: perfect hands are a marked characteristic of a lofty mind. Jesus Christ performed all his miracles by means of his hands. It is through the pores of the hands that life itself passes; and, on whatsoever they touch, the hands leave the mark of a

magic power. Again the hand has a share in all the
delights of love.

. . . The shades of heat and cold to which it is
susceptible are so minute that they escape the notice
of unobservant people altogether; but they may easily
be distinguished by anyone who has made any sort of
study of the anatomy of the feelings in them relative
to life. The hand can be dry, damp, burning, icy, soft,
rough, oily. It can assume a state of palpitation, of
smoothness, of hardness, of softness—in short, the
hand presents an incomprehensible phenomenon
which one is tempted to call the "incarnation of
the soul."

To get in touch with their inner, automatic, manual spontaneity, lovers may want to begin by touching together a single
fingertip and not do anything except feel the sensations. Without "doing" anything or inhibiting themselves, they allow each
other's fingers and hands to do exactly what they want to, feeling just what they actually do feel.

One finds that each finger and every part of one's hand has
a guiding intelligence. If allowed to move as it wants, each part
will act in synchroneity with every part of your partner's body,
conveying love by spontaneous connection. Each of you can
touch, warmly, slowly, delicately, lightly, very slowly, strongly—
it takes strength to touch gently—lovingly, from the viewpoint
of learning to know your lover's body. Not to know it once and
for all, but with each changing moment as your lover's body
changes in response to each touch.

Without making a deliberate effort to do anything at all,
one can simply watch his or her hands begin to touch in countless ways. By the tips of single fingers or with the whole hand,
held loose or firm, flat, cupped, holding, tenderly, teasingly,
front or back, opening and closing, fingers apart or together,
with long continuous stroking, or almost tickling, almost

squeezing, almost pulling—all automatically just the right amount, just the right place, just the right moment, once you let your hands handle it.

It would be as impossible for lovers to direct their fingers and hands to stimulate, to manipulate this or that spot, button, or anatomical switch, as for a pianist to direct each finger to hit each individual key when playing a musical piece. Fortunately, unlike playing a score by someone else, your hands instinctively know all the right notes to play and how to express them lovingly, with feeling for your partner's entire body. You sense your own and your partner's responses throughout your whole body, as both your feelings swell in an endless series of impromptu crescendos, harmonies, rhythms, melodies, volumes, beats, and even lyrics.

One or two hands at once, and/or kissing—it's all touching. So is intercourse; foreplay and intercourse have a lot more in common than they have differences. If lovers are spontaneous, then hugging and kissing, intercourse and foreplay, are all one spontaneous, endless, loving connection. All one long poem.

In the slow-motion Chinese meditation dance called t'ai chi (established, according to tradition, by a Taoist during the Sung dynasty), couples practice what is called pushing hands. Just enough very light contact is maintained with the partner to feel what he or she is doing; then one allows oneself to respond spontaneously to the feeling.

This intuitive responding is true for any partner dancing, in which leading and following are more important keys than the steps or the beat of the music. The steps are vague, global guidelines for getting started in moving to each other's signals by a sense of feel.

The Act

Spontaneity applies to intercourse as well, except that in social dancing the man usually leads, whereas in the sacred dance of lovemaking, either partner may be active or passive, either lead-ing or following, or doing both. The only important step is that lovers participate by allowing it to happen spontaneously, just waiting to feel each body begin to move of its own accord. Then lovers will begin to move together naturally in just the right way for each other, adjusting automatically to what they feel in themselves and from their partners.

The absurdity of talking about different pelvic or any other sexual movements for intercourse is that, although there may be some basic sexual motions, they are defined by the lovers to-gether, united and acting and reacting as one, and usually touching together in many more ways than at the pelvis.

Mystical sex does not occur in a vacuum, nor is it some-thing one does on one's own as a random groping into space or onto one's partner. It is not one partner doing something to, for, at, in, or even with the other. It is each creatively, spontaneously, responding to the other so that the couple acts as one.

The actual motions described in space are unlimited and potentially include any and all technical movements. After all, spontaneous sex emanates from the creative, inventive, artistic side of the human mind, which is why partners make love much, much more creatively without thinking about what to do. Spontaneity is also why mystical sex never gets boring; it is pure, constant, ever-renewed creativity. It is not so much the shape, size, speed, or force of the movements that makes it exciting, but the togetherness promoted between lovers, the inti-macy, the closeness, the connection, a literal, undeniable fact of actual unity in which two lovers have become one single being that feels, reacts, and spontaneously acts as a unified whole.

If a couple makes no effort to perform, move, or otherwise fuck in some particular, deliberate manner, or to inhibit their bodies, by feeling their own and their partner's feelings they will soon find themselves begin to move naturally in a flowing, end-less, effortless, undulating, swaying, rippling wave that carries them along without end. Without effort, one can be transported by the feeling that "it's happening to me," rather than "I'm doing it."

For some, this is startling, even frightening at first, because to ride along on this sacred wave is to begin to enter into mystical experience. One no longer merely senses the pleasures of sexual excitement, but realizes an altered state of mind, an ineffable feeling and understanding about one's relationship to the whole of the cosmos. It is a feeling that words cannot describe. This is real spontaneity.

The best part of spontaneity, and all of mystical sex, is that unless we prevent it, it happens naturally, automatically, effortlessly, even for those couples for whom sex has been awkward, clumsy, foolish, spastic, embarrassing, ignorant, nonexistent, and generally a mess. Even the partner who has been uncoordinated, insensitive, anxious, squeamish, indelicate, and afraid will realize an innate ability to make contact lovingly, patiently, gently, playfully, erotically, and above all, naturally. Mystical sex is not a more difficult discipline than regular sex. It's not a skill we need to practice. It is an ability and an awareness that everyone is born with. We can all, spontaneously, learn to allow it to happen for us.

Integration of the Three Elements of Mystical Sex

Translators and commentators on mysticism have never clearly connected the three characteristics of mystical sex: timelessness, a meditative state of mind, and spontaneity. We may suppose that these writers misunderstood one or more of the three elements. For example, coitus reservatus was often confused with orgasmless sex, "not thinking" was frequently misunderstood as having a blank mind, and "contain breath" was generally mistaken for a lung exercise.

In *Yoga: Immortality and Freedom*, Mircea Eliade stated, "The underlying idea was the necessity of achieving simultaneous 'immobility' of breath, thought, and semen." But he did not say how or why they were related. Similarly, the ancient Tantric text, *Goraksa Samhita*, stated: "So long as breath is in motion, the semen moves also. When breath ceases to move, the semen is also at rest. . . . When the breath moves, the mind moves also; when the breath ceases to move, the mind becomes motionless." But, again, there is no coherent explanation as to how or why these aspects of mystical sex go together.

Some writers insinuate that the connection is sentimental, vague, or symbolic. Others have proposed that one of the three aspects is merely a part or subset of another. They speak, for example, of breath control being a part of or a method of practicing coitus reservatus, a sort of auxiliary technique. This was a common mistake.

But if one understands each of the three elements individually, their many interrelationships are clear. Let us list a few of the connections in an attempt to give a feeling for how timelessness, mental absorption, and spontaneity go together in mystical sex. These connections occur on several different levels, including the biological, functional, and temporal planes.

On a biological level, the characteristics of mystical sex are organically linked in that all are associated with the right hemisphere of the brain. Mystical sex is making love from the right side of the mind.

Conversely, on a functional level, we will naturally make love from the right side of the brain unless we are overpowered by activity associated with the left hemisphere: conceptual, verbal thought, and deliberate, mission-oriented behavior. On the verbal level, the characteristics of mystical sex were often defined in terms of a negation of those left-brain functions.

On a temporal level, all three elements of mystical sex involve a complete immersion in the immediate present moment of time. Direct sensory awareness is how we experience the present. Our immediate perceptions *are* the present. Spontaneity is our unhesitating reaction *in* the present. It is a simultaneous involvement with what is actually going on, rather than with what we are imagining. In this way, spontaneity and direct awareness are the same as what is meant by timelessness in coitus reservatus.

In coitus reservatus, one lies outside of time by one's absorption in the present moment, which is direct sensory awareness. That same awareness provides one the immediate feedback of sensation that allows one to continue making love, so that sex is without end, that is, not constrained or limited by time. Or, we could say that direct perception enables spontaneous action, in which lovers make love without end, by virtue of being immersed in the immediate present moment, which is the same as one's direct perceptions, which is where we just started.

We begin to realize that we are chasing our own tails in a circle, and we can go on identifying connections because the three elements, aspects, or characteristics have to go together. They are not so much different entities, but simply different ways of talking about the same experience of mystical sex. For the same reason, we can't have one without the others: They don't cause each other; they arise mutually and together as integral parts of a bigger picture, as do the heat, light, and gravity of the sun.

How Mystical Sex "Causes" Mystical Experience

Another element arises naturally in mystical sex: the transportation of consciousness to the subtle, transpersonal plane of experience.

Earlier, I listed several ways in which authors have tried to write about that ineffable, altered state of mind called mystical experience. It has been called a paranormal consciousness, compared with other states such as dreaming or floating, and described as a timeless, and even a religious, dimension of experience. It has strong parallels with feelings of love, or being in love.

But what "causes" mystical experience to come about? Answers to this question are generally either given in microcosmic, subpersonal terms, or in macrocosmic, transpersonal terms. The symbolic explanation of human nature on both microcosmic and macrocosmic levels—that is, from the point of view of the smaller elements that make up man, as well as the larger context of which man is a part—is typical of the mystical literature's emphasis on proportion, and is an example of the mystical dictum, "As above, so below." Mystical philosophy contains a microcosmic and a macrocosmic correlate to every phenomenon, in lieu of speaking in terms of cause and effect. Let us look at these two ways of explaining how mystical experience comes about.

The Microcosmic View

Sexual feelings have been attributed by medicine to various subpersonal, that is, biochemical or bioelectric substances or energies, such as hormones, magnetism, and electricity.

Psychiatrist Wilhelm Reich spoke of a mysterious fluid force he called orgone as the essence of sexual feelings. Several medical and popular writers around the turn of the century spoke of animal or social magnetism, as in Margaret Sanger's *Magnetation Methods of Birth Control*. Recent authors on yoga have theorized that a spinal tap would reveal the presence of a "sex essence" that becomes operant during sex. Dr. Rudolph von Urban proposed that when a man and woman join sexually, they establish something akin to the two poles of a magnet or battery, creating an electrical force field and facilitating a bio-electrical streaming of energy between the two bodies—a sub-personal mechanism of action à deux.

Such theoretical propositions have yet to be substantiated, even though we would expect that they could be tested rather easily.

On a more likely note, in *The Chemistry of Love*, Dr. Michael Leibowitz suggested that a "naturally occurring amphetamine-like substance" and other "drugs within us" may be responsible for tranquil or high feelings—a kind of sexual version of the aerobic, neuroendocrine release of natural opiates associated with calisthenics or jogging. Along these same lines, Edward and Jeremy Brecker, chroniclers of modern sex re-search, summarized several studies that showed how sexual arousal, even without orgasm and even without coitus, signifi-cantly raised blood levels of the sex hormones including testos-terone. Furthermore, researchers have reported a large increase in electrical activity in the right brain hemisphere during the time prior to orgasm and terminating at that point.

While some of these findings may seem very relevant, they offer more of a description of what occurs than a satisfactory explanation of why one feels an altered state of mind. Of course we would expect there to be some kind of biologic change asso-ciated with a change in one's state of mind; it would be surpris-ing, shocking really, if there were no physical correlates what-soever with an elevation of consciousness.

The mystical traditions also proposed a symbolic, pseudo-neurochemical description of consciousness being elevated. A common explanation, shared by all the major mystical tradi-tions, East and West, described consciousness as being stimu-lated, then elevated, through different planes or levels in the body, finally even ending up outside the body, above the head.

Taoism, Tantrism, Gnosticism, Alchemy, and Kabbalism all had virtually the same explanation of how mystical experience works, including illustrations of this symbolic action. Figure 4 shows how the Kabbalists and Tantrists pictured consciousness being conveyed through a number of subpersonal stages. In Taoism the essence rises, in Tantrism the kundalini ascends, in Gnosticism the River Jordan flows uphill, in Kabbalism the lightning flashes, and in the Alchemy of East and West the basest metal, lead, is transformed into the highest, gold. Such pictures and explanations were also used to symbolize key elements of mystical philosophy; that is, they were aids to remembering basic mystical ideas, one of the most important of which is the conjunction of opposites.

Unfortunately, many authors on yoga-meditation have misunderstood this mystic symbolism of elevated consciousness to be a sort of medical treatise on human anatomy and physiology. They have consequently described and discussed among themselves a variety of "subtle" organs and substances, which in reality simply don't exist, any more than gold can actually be manufactured from lead. When the third century A.D. Taoist alchemist said, "'Made gold' is better than natural gold," he didn't mean that synthetic gold is purer than mined gold; he meant that a transcendental state of mind is better than money.

The Macrocosmic View

Just as there is a microcosmic component to mystical experience, so, too, there is a macrocosmic, transpersonal explanation of why one reaches transcendence during mystical sex.

According to this view, a man and woman making love form a new synergistic entity. This new being has qualities and a cosmic relevance that could not be predicted, understood, or accounted for by the simple addition of the characteristics of the two lovers separately, just as neither hydrogen nor oxygen alone has the qualities of water until the two are combined.

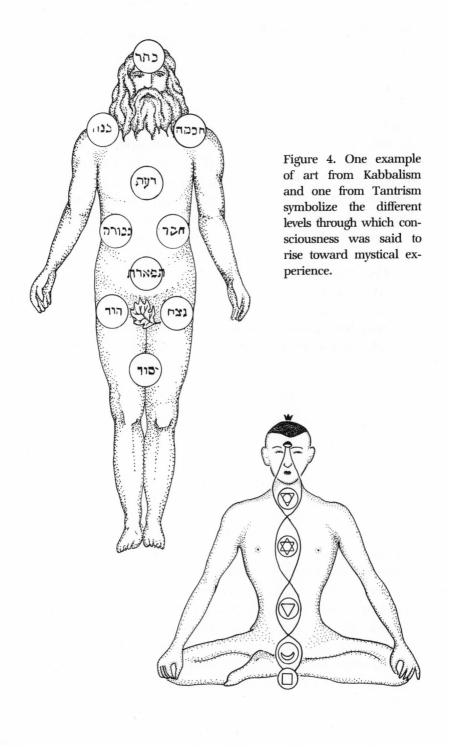

Figure 4. One example of art from Kabbalism and one from Tantrism symbolize the different levels through which consciousness was said to rise toward mystical experience.

One by-product of a sexually combined man and woman, so this story goes, is mystical consciousness.

Greek, Hebrew, Indian, and Chinese mystical literature provided a macrocosmic explanation of mystical experience in the myth of the hermaphrodites, a race of beings who were both male and female in one. In Plato's version, they were so powerful that the gods decided to break them into male and female, with the memory of their earlier state and the impulse to reconstitute that earlier condition. In this vision, then, a man or woman is only half a human being, and reaches wholeness only when unified with the other. In *The Zohar*, Ariel Bension recounted the Kabbalist version of this principle:

> "The world," said the Master, "rests upon the union of the male and the female principle. That form in which we do not find both the male and the female principle is neither a complete nor superior form."
>
> Before coming to this earth, each soul and each spirit is composed of a man and a woman, united in one single being. On coming down to earth the two halves are separated and sent to animate two different bodies.

This macrocosmic explanation of mystical sex was central to the mystical theme of the conjunction of opposites, whereby the unity of all things is realized, despite the differences and separations we ordinarily focus on. Human lovemaking symbolizes a cosmic coming together, a conjunction and resolution of differences, by means of opposites joining to form a larger whole. In Eliade's words from *Yoga: Immortality and Freedom*, "The conjunction of opposites constitutes the metaphysical constant of all Tantric rituals and meditation."

In Taoism, the joining of yin and yang, the male principle and the female principle, exemplifies the same point, the interdependence and relativity of opposites or, more correctly, of complements. In Gnosticism, according to Marvin Meyer in *The Ancient Mysteries*, "The highest sacrament is the bridal chamber, the 'true mystery' by means of which one transcends the divisions that separate Adam and Eve, man from woman, and the divine from the human." Alchemy uses exactly the same term, conjunction of opposites. Stanislaus De Rola writes in *Alchemy*, "Conjunction or perfect solution: The two bodies are made one as they dissolve into the liquid [mystical] state."

The illustration in Figure 5 symbolizes the chemical wedding or alchemical marriage, in which lovers represent the unity of king and queen, sun and moon, male and female, and every other kind of pair ordinarily thought of as opposites.

Of course, all of us are always joined to the cosmos by our breathing, eating, gravity, air pressure, and so on, but we can nevertheless easily feel isolated from the rest of the universe. However, in lovemaking we can let ourselves realize and know our literal, transubstantial connection with the outside world, with what is usually thought of as "not me." Perhaps we can say, from a workable, practical perspective, that it is this intimacy, the physical and mental bonding that is unavoidable in timeless, spontaneous lovemaking, that promotes an altered state. In a sense, coitus reservatus forces lovers to be intimate on every level.

Sexual love is in fact a joining, unity, conjunction, and yoga (all four words come from the same root) through which a man and a woman actually become not only close, but part of each other. They can experience an elevation of their psychological plane precisely because of this "paradoxical, inexpressible experience of the discovery of Unity," the ultimate intimacy with each other.

This intimacy can extend throughout one's relationship, beyond sexuality and into the realm of love. For this reason, when a man and woman are limerantly and affectionately in love, they pass the day and night in the floating, transcendent,

Figure 5. An illustration from Alchemy represents one concept of the conjunction of opposites: the alchemical marriage.

dreamy plane, because they have bonded on a psychological, cosmic level and they feel as one, even when they are not in each other's presence.

However we symbolize or interpret it, the macrocosmic vision of mystical experience, like the microcosmic, is a description of what happens rather than an explanation of how or why mystical experience is realized. Again, mystical philosophy rejects the simple cause-effect schema for explaining nature.

Why do we ask how mystical sex causes mystical experience? After all, we don't ask what causes the official four stages of sexual response. They are simply assumed to be the natural course of the human sexual response cycle, as described by Dr. Albert Moll and others around the turn of the century, and popularized by Masters and Johnson in 1966.

At the outset of their *Human Sexual Response*, Masters and Johnson stated that their techniques of defining and describing sexual response were "primarily those of direct observation and physical measurement." To their credit, they reported what goes on without trying to overanalyze each change according to cause and effect.

But mystical experience is not included in medicine's classic description of human sexual response, so we are led to wonder what "unusual" factors cause this mystical reaction that is perceived as special or out of the ordinary. In reality, as with the other elements of mystical sex, mystical experience can be a natural, normal part of lovemaking, which will occur unless it is prevented, blocked, or interfered with by one's attitude and approach to sex.

The real question is not, what causes mystical experience? but, what prevents it? We have identified these obstacles—covert verbal self-talk, deliberate mission-oriented behavior, and other factors associated with left hemisphere hyperactivity. Simply letting go of them allows mystical experience to occur naturally.

5

Mystical Marriage

"Make yourself *attractive* to the other sex by making yourself *opposite* from the other sex." The problem? Opposites attract; they just can't live together. Sex-role training becomes divorce training.

> *Why Men Are the Way They Are*
> WARREN FARRELL

We are not the same persons this year as last; nor are those we love. It is a happy chance if we, changing, continue to love a changed person.

> *The Summing Up*
> W. SOMERSET MAUGHAM

THE WEDDING CEREMONY IS A HOLDOVER FROM ANCIENT times when priests were paid to bless a wide range of social events and occasions. Even the routine slaughter of livestock necessitated a performance by a clergyman, who would conduct a good-luck sacrifice, that is, a make-believe tributary offering to demonstrate fealty and otherwise placate a totalitarian and often hotheaded cosmic ruler.

Of course, sacrifices have been abandoned by civilized peoples, not because they are evil or bad, but because they are a waste of time; they don't work, or even help. But the tradition of a marriage is still so deeply ingrained that every male-female bonding is seen automatically in a ceremonial context. Two people can't just be a couple; they are either married or unmarried.

Today's concepts of marriage and weddings have developed over time and are based on a number of cultural, political, and theological factors. Despite changes in our attitudes about sex roles, sexual behavior, morality, relationships, and the family, we still cling to beliefs about marriage that stem from religiolegal marriage of ancient times, romantic love born in the tradition of chivalry, and a collection of traditions that form a vague, generic image of marriage today. These traditions also serve as a contrast to the concept of mystical marriage.

In mysticism, male-female unity, equality, and monogamy were viewed as part of natural, not man-made or religious, law. This was historically symbolized, for example, by the mystical themes of androgyny, the Platonic and Kabbalistic hermaphrodite, and Alchemy's chemical wedding or alchemical marriage, in which the elements of nature bonded to become new synergistic entities. Mystical marriage is a natural marriage of the male and female aspects of two individuals (in the same way that water is the mystical "marriage" of hydrogen and oxygen). It occurs entirely independent of social custom or other symbolic labeling. The two become naturally part of a unity, a greater partnership, not because they signed a piece of paper or were blessed by a professional clergyman or a justice-of-the-peace, but because it is their most natural state of being.

Conversely, if two people are not suited to each other, no vows, pronouncements, or ceremonies will help. They will be volatile and at times dangerously unstable as long as they stay together. As such, the mystical marriage corresponds to the actual, tangible reality of how a man and woman feel and act toward each other, as distinct from what the relationship is on paper, or what it is verbally pronounced to be by religious or political authorities.

Mystical marriage is an organic contrast to the externally imposed roles of the religious and legal institutions of marriage. And technically, in referring to mystical marriage, we are not really talking about formal marriage at all, but of any monogamous, ongoing love relationship in or out of regular marriage. Mystical marriage could even include a homosexual relationship, although this chapter will speak in terms of a man-woman partnership.

Because mysticism emphasizes a mode of thinking or consciousness, its applications to a love relationship are potentially innumerable. One can experience and engage in every aspect of an intimate partnership from the mystical side of the mind, using that mode of consciousness associated with sensation, feeling, creative spontaneity, and the right hemisphere of the brain. For practical reasons then, we must limit our focus to a few aspects of the mystical male-female relationship, while trying to gain a larger, overall attitude applicable to a monogamous love partnership.

Considering the difficulties of marriage, some social commentators have wondered why as many marriages stay together as actually do. But from a mystical point of view, those successful couples and families would almost invariably have stayed together whether or not the man and woman were formally married at all. In fact, since nearly all couples who are about to be married feel happy and loving, while more than half will subsequently decide to separate and divorce, we could even reason that marriage *causes* male-female partnerships to fall apart.

The popular theologies argue that society must help a man and woman stay together by the symbolic social bond of marriage, without which couples would naturally separate. The correlary of this reasoning is: If we didn't have rules and laws against premarital sex, oral sex, homosexuality, adultery, public exposure, bestiality, and incest, people would naturally behave promiscuously, indiscriminately, and weirdly. In this view, monogamy is merely promiscuity in slow time, a partnership held in desperate check by fear of legal or cosmic punishment. In other words, religiopolitical authority infers that there is something against the grain of human nature about monogamy and the family unit, which therefore needs the helping hand of a marriage to preserve.

Mysticism rejects this image, and contends that adult human beings are most in tune with their own human nature when paired as man and woman—with or without an official, religiolegal state of marriage. By claiming that marriage keeps families together, religious and political authorities are attempting to take credit for something that would happen automatically anyway.

To use the analogy of the chemical reaction, when the elements of sodium and chlorine combine to make table salt, they do so whether or not we pronounce them "married," or "salt," say "abracadabra," or file a piece of paper, or do anything else on a verbal-symbolic level. On the other hand, oil and water do not mix, whether or not words are pronounced by authorities or written down or referred to from a sacred book.

In mystical marriage, partners engage in an ongoing attempt to know themselves and each other, consciously deciding exactly what they want their partnership to be, and taking full responsibility for their decisions. It is always an equal partnership, an ever-evolving partnership, with the personal growth of each partner as an individual as the goal and purpose of the marriage.

The same primacy of the individual and of personal decision gave form to mysticism's historic association with democracy and individual freedom on a sociopolitical level. In democracy, the people choose what their government will be. In mystical marriage, the couple chooses what its partnership will be. Each mystical marriage is uniquely what the couple decides for itself the relationship will become. Lovers take responsibility for making their partnership evolve as they want it to, using the intuitive, intimately shared creativity that comes from their hearts as autonomous individuals.

In Table 3, we can compare four approaches to marriage: the historic religiolegal marriage, the chivalrous stereotype of male-female romance, today's generic marriage based on centuries of tradition, and the mystical marriage. The table indicates the differing approaches to courtship, legal contract, political relationship, property, role, sex, love, delusions inherent in each sort of marriage, their historic relevance, and the nature of the wedding ceremony in each form of relationship.

Arranged Marriage

Even though most couples don't think much about what they want in a relationship, Western culture has moved in a mystical direction, in that husband and wife now choose each other. This is quite a remarkable contrast to the arranged marriage, which was the custom of the Western world until recent times, and

Table 3

Mystical Marriage Compared to Other
Forms of Relationship

TYPES OF RELATIONSHIPS	COURTSHIP	LEGAL CONTRACT	POLITICAL RELATIONSHIP	PROPERTY
HISTORIC RELIGIOLEGAL MARRIAGE	Arranged by families	Man buys woman	Man owns woman	Husband legally acquires all of wife's property
CHIVALROUS ROMANTIC LOVE	Love at first sight	None: Marriage considered legalized fornication	Woman placed above man	Man voluntarily gives everything to woman
TRADITIONAL OR GENERIC MARRIAGE	Man and woman choose each other after period of romantic role-playing	Marriage law ignored or accepted uncritically	Man as benign dictator, protecting woman	Woman legally acquires half of man's income, savings; aborts her own career
MYSTICAL MARRIAGE	Spontaneous honesty in revealing self and learning to know the other	Formulated and agreed upon by the couple	Man and woman equal partners in all matters	Both partners strive for financial self-sufficiency

DAILY ROLE	SEX	LOVE	DELUSIONS	HISTORIC RELEVANCE	WEDDING CEREMONY
Woman serves man	Fertilization for production of heirs; his venereal gratification	Coincidental if it exists at all in marriage; arranged for on the side by husband	Supernatural beings will take care of the relationship	Perpetuation of patriarchal system	Magic words pronounced by authority
Man serves woman	Idealization; mystical sex	Arranged for on the side by wife	Love will take care of the relationship	Rebellion against female servitude and caste systems	None
Man works at job for money, woman works for man, and children for no pay	Sex legalized by marriage; outside marriage it is fornication	Love fades; commitment picks up slack	Marriage will take care of the relationship	Refusal to acknowledge need for social change	Traditional ritual
Personal growth toward greater love and autonomy	Love; mystical sex	Ever-evolving unity from growth of each partner	Conscious attempt to avoid or correct one's delusions about self, other, relationship, cosmos	Social evolution toward harmony with nature	Decided on by couple

which is still operant in Hindu and Muslim cultures. Indeed, until relatively modern history, love—especially romantic love—and marriage were looked upon as separate entities.

Marriages were arranged by families—often for the acquisition of the wife's family's property, a practice later customized as the dowry. Love, when it was acknowledged at all, was often arranged for on the side, usually by the husband. Husband and wife were not expected to start out loving each other, except by amusing chance. They stayed together by a commitment to social custom and because divorce was often extremely difficult or impossible to obtain, as it still is in many cultures regardless of how barbaric, how inhuman a marriage becomes.

However, we cannot say that it was only the severity of divorce law that held couples together under the system of arranged marriage. Many became happy, healthy, loving, and successful marriages; this transformation attests to, if nothing else, the flexibility and ability of mentally healthy men and women to adapt to each other.

Today, when getting married, we choose our spouses. We often choose poorly, perhaps not as well as our parents could have chosen for us. Though we marry for love, we often have an unclear vision of what love is.

Chivalry and Romantic Love

In the Middle Ages, Chivalry in the East and West spoke out in various ways against the brutality of marriage. The literature of European Chivalry, including the songs of the troubadours and the Arthurian romances, formalized a disdain for the prevailing view of marriage and its schema for male-female relationships, which they sought to replace with their new arrangement, that of romantic love. The chivalrous attitudes about love spread from India and Persia to Spain and France, and were expressed in several recurrent themes. For example, the popular theme of a man loving a married woman was used to establish that love and marriage were separate entities.

Chivalry has bequeathed to us some aspects of mystical love and mystical sex and the tradition of marrying for love. But it has also engendered some unrealistic myths about love and romance that work against a couple's ability to know each other.

The caricature of Chivalry is the love of the unattainable lady, worshiped from afar. Psychologically, this is often seen still in the way partners idealize each other, imagining the partner has qualities that aren't really there, or ignoring problems the partner actually does have. Lovers may live together, but know each other only as they imagine each other as if from a distance.

Rejecting the Christian view of sex that equated lovemaking and fertilization, Chivalry recommended coitus reservatus and mystical sex, as portrayed by René Nelli in his fascinating *Erotique des Troubadours.* And de Rougemont explained:

> *The cultivation of passionate love began in Europe as a reaction to Christianity (and in particular to its doctrine of marriage).* . . .
>
> That all European poetry has come out of Provençal poetry written in the 12th century by the troubadours of Languedoc is now accepted on every side. . . .
>
> No European poetry has been more profoundly *rhetorical,* not only in its verbal and musical forms . . . in its actual inspiration which it obtained from a fixed system of rules which was codified as the *leys d'amor.* . . . What it quickens with noble emotion is love outside marriage; for marriage implies no more than a physical union, but 'Amor'—the supreme Eros—is the transport of the soul upwards to ultimate union.

As an artistic-literary motif, these troubadour laws or keys of love are still with us to this day, and serve as the backdrop of the plot line for much of Western culture's highest achievements in opera, theater, and cinema, as well as for soap operas, men's and women's magazines, and the so-called romance novel—among the best-selling literature in the world. The romantic view of men and women is at the core of the current psychology of product advertising in our free market economy.

During this Age of Chivalry, the literary courts of love debated questions about male-female relationships. Debate consisted of humorous repartee blending what J. Huizinga called the "baldest sensualism with refined mysticism." In the courts of love, marriage was called *iuriata fornicatio*: legalized sex, sex sanctioned and under the control of religious and political authority.

Chivalry's mystical theme of male-female equality yielded many common-sense recommendations such as patience, sincerity, loyalty, gazing, speaking, touching, kissing, and, above all, love. But, although such romantic courting behaviors, based on the codes of chivalry, can enhance a relationship, they are often merely acted out by couples who are sexually seducing each other en route to a religiolegal marriage or, later, "on the side" of one.

But we must remember that while the historic appearance of Chivalry in Europe did represent a mystical movement, its stereotype of romantic love was a deliberately satirical and melodramatic exaggeration of a mystical marriage. If taken literally it is an example of a marital role widely known as idealization, in which the partners love, not each other, but their idealized images of themselves and each other.

Today how do a man and a woman know they are choosing the "right" partner to marry? They feel what they assume is love. They feel a transcendental, altered state of mind, and a unity with each other. Indeed, the feelings of unity and being "in love" are two of the allusions often used to describe mystical experience.

But those transcendental high feelings between a man and a woman can be brought about not only by love and mystical sex, but by psychological unions in which man and woman bond emotionally because they reciprocate each other's emotional disorders. As in mathematics, the reciprocals make one, but it is often a neurotic, not a loving, spiritual compatibility. Nevertheless, because it is a bonding and a high feeling, this limerance is taken as a sign that they should marry each other.

Commitment

Two people meet each other, feel strong pleasurable emotions, an attraction, a unity, a wish to be together. They go out of their way to be on their best, most romantic behavior, they have similar interests or some other recreational affinity, they think they love each other. Therefore they get married. This is puerile and ultimately tragic. In Balzac's words, "They speak of love as a slave speaks of freedom." For a couple to decide to marry because they feel a blissful transcendental bond with each other, whether based on sex, idealization, some individual psychic defense, a symbiotic complementarity of their emotional problems, or actual love, would be comical if it were not the colloquial rule.

Such "love" can even become detrimental to fidelity as when a spouse experiences similar loving feelings and attraction for someone outside of marriage. Or when one partner feels compelled to leave a relationship if he or she loses those feelings that felt like love. In fifteen years of doing marital therapy, the comment I have heard most frequently has been, "We thought we loved each other, but we didn't really know each other." In contrast, mystical marriage is based on knowing, as well as loving, each other.

Who were these spouses in love with, to begin with? An image of one person was in love with an image of that other person, with the role the other was playing, not the real person. It was a conceptual, imaginary marriage, not a mystical marriage, even if there was a formal legal or religious ceremony.

Yes, of course, say the authorities, love fades. A couple stays together by commitment. In this way, today's free-will marriage based on love becomes an arranged marriage, preserved by social commitment. The marriage freely entered into appears, in retrospect, to have been arranged by the persons the man and woman imagined each other to be. Not only have they become different people, for better or for worse, but too often they realize that they didn't even know themselves when they made their free-will choice of each other.

Certainly commitment is a vital part of a successful relationship (or any worthwhile endeavor). But there is an important difference between a commitment to one's lover, made because each partner wants to make that determination to work things out, and a compulsive, unfeeling, mechanical commitment to the theoretical institution of marriage, made because couples believe they should stay together because of external religious or social rules.

Traditional or Generic Marriage

Today partners expect love and marriage to go together. But what do they expect from a love relationship? It is shocking how little thought men and women give to this question. Instead they too often look at marriage as an institution, like school, into which everyone enters at a certain age, continuing or dropping out, depending on how things are going at any given point.

Couples very often make fewer, less detailed plans for their marriage, for the nuts and bolts of living together, relating maturely and lovingly to each other, parenting, and growing emotionally as individuals, than they do for the one day of their wedding. For this ceremony people who may already be in debt will spend large sums of money, thinking that this beautiful "statement to the world" is going to improve their fate.

Surely, marriage is a nice tradition, one that will link the experience of generations, foster a sense of history and continuity, promote a healthy, if theatrical, sense of awe and respect for ritual ceremony, and otherwise bring about a nostalgic delight by virtue of long custom, if nothing else. But many people confuse social tradition with traditional religious ritual, a sympathetic magic supposedly brought into requisition by a properly executed wedding ceremony—particular words and gestures, spoken and performed in an established sequence by a recognized theologic authority. Invariably common to all popular religious authorities is the pompous and fanciful assertion that couples will derive supernatural favoritism, good luck in marital life, and protection from sinister forces, as long as they are officially married, as opposed to "living in sin."

Relying on either the nostalgia of a nice tradition or the supernatural, magic effect of a religious ritual for the success of a relationship not only ignores the facts. It also lulls a couple into a false security, complacency if not boredom, an ignorance that does not encourage the couple to take full responsibility for the direction of their partnership, but compels them instead to unconsciously motivated behaviors. Among these behaviors are the roles assigned to each spouse by traditions of marital life going back centuries.

Marital Roles

Traditional marital roles for each partner are concepts. They may reflect imagined pictures and verbal descriptions that religion, law, parents, and society say marriage is supposed to be.

Or, they can include fantasy idealizations one imagines a partner is or isn't or will become, or roles may be based on an unrealistic image of oneself. Consequently they become an unconscious programming of one's behavior. Because roles are conceptual, they reflect a mode of consciousness associated with the left hemisphere of the brain.

I have mentioned how drawing in an artistic way is a question of seeing the subject as it actually is rather than how we conceptualize it; how spontaneity in sex involves feeling what we are actually feeling, unclouded by our thoughts about what is happening; and how science is an attitude toward the cosmos, based on direct observation of nature, rather than a fixed body of knowledge. In the same way, a mystical marriage involves an honest, intuitive spontaneity between oneself and one's partner, and it is an ongoing evolution of that couple's understanding of each other. Conversely, the couple strives to avoid acting toward each other according to hidden, internal scenarios and motivations, conscious or unconscious. By learning to recognize these roles and images, they learn to avoid them.

Roles, preprogrammed instructions, agendas, or "games people play" often arise from the various forms of left-brain concepts through which we filter and distort our understanding of ourselves and of the world around us, including our love relationships. Roles, and the effects they have on us, vary according to the combination of words and images on the computer screens of our left hemisphere mode of consciousness. They correspond loosely with the sorts of psychological or emotional disturbances we observe in individuals. Many are hidden from one's partner; others are unconscious, hidden from oneself.

One male-female role game is expounded upon by Warren Farrell in his very enlightening *Why Men Are the Way They Are*. Farrell detailed the differing socially enculturated concepts—he called them primary and secondary fantasies—that motivate male and female attractiveness toward each other and toward marriage.

Farrell systematically and very persuasively examined how women are indeed still "sex objects" because men's primary fantasy is sexual access to beautiful women. At the same time, men are shown to be "success objects" because women's primary fantasy is financial security (especially a home and family) without having to work if she doesn't want to. This accounts for women's hyperobsession with their appearance, and men's with power and money, Farrell says. It parallels Ogden Nash's quip that a little incompatibility is good for a marriage "as long as he has income, and she has patability." What is obscured is that this arrangement perpetuates the male's superior situation in socioeconomic terms.

Although thoughtful men and women don't embrace these ideas on a conscious level, to one degree or another they are very much a part of many individuals' internal thinking. Their awareness of these motivations is held inside, not expressed, a hidden agenda that is acted out, sometimes throughout an entire marriage, or until the roles wear thin and divorce sets in.

What is perpetuated by social fantasies and taboos expressed through mass media and traditional institutions is a system in which men and women are attracted, not emotionally to each other as people, but for the roles they play and the fantasies they fulfill in the imagination of their left brain hemisphere mode of consciousness. The result, warns Farrell, is that "sex role training becomes divorce training."

Subjugation of Women

Another holdover of historical marriage is the popular acceptance of the Victorian notion that marriage somehow "protects" women. This argument is perfectly analogous to the rationalization—very widespread and sincere at one time—that the institution of slavery provided food and shelter and otherwise protected slaves. In reality, today's social roles, including marriage, render many women helpless, dependent, and unable to fend for themselves. The traditional marriage causes rather than solves the problems of personal autonomy and self-sufficiency in women, as Collette Dowling detailed in her compelling *The Cinderella Complex*. In this respect, we are moving backwards, for the law no longer even provides compensation for a woman's years or decades of homemaking and raising children, as it once did.

Historically, the mystical traditions have opposed the statutory paper contract called marriage because it embodied, formalized, and enforced the actual, legal subjugation of women and their ownership by men, a role system put in place by the patriarchal Indo-Europeans and Semites at least four thousand years ago.

Reflecting Semitic law around 500 B.C., one of the first chapters in the Bible quotes God as claiming that He put enmity between man and woman (Genesis 3:15), and that the husband shall rule over the wife (Genesis 3:16). This attitude was later operant in Roman law, under which the husband held the power of life and death over his wife. And it was well after A.D. 1500 that the Catholic Church recognized women as fully human beings with souls. As in other forms of servitude, women themselves were not legally considered *persons*— that's why women and slaves could never vote. In the eyes of the law, women were *property*, sold by their fathers, then owned by their husbands according to the sales contract called marriage; hence, adultery was treated as an infringement on the man's property rights.

In many cases, common human decency and compassion kept marriage from being unnecessarily cruel or sadistic. And women's rights did fluctuate widely, according to the level of civilization a given society had attained, as did racial slavery.

But this was little consolation to individual women or women in general.

This basic legal meaning of marriage was carried along past the turn of this century, although the rights of women had always been enhanced during the principal mystical reflowerings, for example, in classic Greece, the Age of Chivalry, and the Enlightenment.

Today, we bask in the afterglow of the Enlightenment. Of course, things are better now, in the westernized world. But it has been less than one average lifetime since women were politically emancipated, "given" the vote. This revolutionary turning point has occurred so recently in a historic sense that Western social consciousness has barely even begun to be successfully restructured. Indeed, the vast majority of men in the world still do not have the vote either.

Nevertheless, the fact that Western women are no longer the chattel, the movable property, of their husbands contains the very real danger that the previous four thousand years will be obscured or forgotten. Not only is the past already ignored by many, but so is the fate of women in the rest of the world *today*. A huge portion of the world's women are still legally enslaved to men. In Moslem countries, polygamy, among other degradations, is legal. Hindu culture is little better, despite India's laws to the contrary. And, although it is officially illegal, in many regions of China, peasants still literally buy wives—they feel it "saves money and trouble," says one governmental article. In recent years, according to a *New York Times* report, well over fifty thousand women have been abducted, transported far from home, and sold. They have little or no chance of escape. To this day, a shocking number of young Moslem and black African females undergo infibulation, or clitoral amputation, to render them more docile, domesticated, better able to later serve their husband-masters. Eric Hansen, author of *Stranger in the Forest*, says there are still literally millions of such cases.

Erotification of Misogeny

Even in America today, by conservative estimates, roughly one-quarter to one-third of all females experience sexual molestation prior to the age of consent, and/or rape or attempted rape at least once as adults, and/or serious violence from their husbands, according to Catherine MacKinnon. Less than 10 percent of women report no sexual assault or harassment in their lives.

No one knows exactly how we choose our partners or how we develop our sense of erotic style, excitement, and what turns us on sexually. What makes people heterosexual or homosexual, promiscuous, monogamous, sexually phobic, or turned on by certain acts, things, or relationships? We know that there does exist a feeling often called sexual chemistry, which reflects a sexual orientation or a style of eroticism. Although it seems to operate almost on a physical, biochemical level, it very often has to do with the *relationship* one has with whoever or whatever turns him or her on.

One widespread type of relationship often associated with erotic feeling has to do with male dominance and female submissiveness. Various writers, including Catherine MacKinnon, have implied that this is our culture's most pervasive eroticism, and hence the basis of pornography, prostitution, rape, the sexual molestation of youngsters, sexual harassment on the job, as well as spouse abuse and codependence. These abuses, one or more of which affects almost every woman in America, are examples of our cultural erotification of misogyny. These ubiquitous forms of woman bashing are associated with erotic feeling, and thus become permanent fixtures, the social giving rise to the personal, the personal perpetuating the social. MacKinnon points out: "Women learn to sexualize powerlessness through experiencing their sexuality under conditions of powerlessness."

One might hope that a cure for such a disorder of eroticism, on a personal and cultural level, is the practice of mystical sex, in or out of marriage. What better way to recondition one's love and excitement than in endless, spontaneous intimacy? How better for lovers to relate sincerely as human beings than in a timeless, trancelike unity?

A genuine emancipation of women and de-erotification of female subservience may require major cultural changes worldwide. These changes could be part of a greater movement toward principles of mystical harmony with the cosmos. Such changes would include the dismantling of the world's organized religions, including organized pseudo-science; the institution of democratic governments throughout the planet; the use of technology to help rather than to pervert ecologic evolution, including the evolution of human consciousness; and, above all, the unqualified political emancipation of women on a global basis. What better time will there be for humanity to embark on the historic cosmic return from civilization based on left hemisphere domination to one that cultivates a balance, a harmonious unity between the two sides of our minds? If nothing else, each mystical marriage is a step on this larger journey, one which began many thousands of years ago, and will continue long into the next millennium.

Divorce

The current utter disintegration of the family and consequent social anarchy are not so much a result of traditional concepts of marriage and sex roles as of our denial of them. The numbers speak—shriek—for themselves. Marriage as a social institution is a disaster: More than half of all marriages will end in divorce, and many, many more would if economic circumstances permitted.

Fifty percent of all first marriages are so intolerable that they end in divorce, and for second and third marriages there is an even higher rate. We say they fail. But is a marriage a success simply by its continuation? What fraction are happy and healthy? Is a marriage in which the husband occasionally rapes, beats, or emotionally degrades the wife and/or the children a success if it doesn't end in divorce? Is a couple that stays together a success if it does so only because one or the other, not to mention the children, would face the specter of poverty, hunger, cold, and endless other suffering and humiliation if alone? How about the couple traumatized by drugs or alcohol?

Is a marriage in which one or both spouses have lovers on the side a success as long as there's no divorce? And how about married couples who have little or no sex at all? Divorce itself is just an external, visible sign of the inner collapse and chaotic disintegration of marriage as a social arrangement, a catastrophe we refuse to fully acknowledge.

It is not divorce that breaks up couples and families. Divorce is simply the name we give to the state of a marital relationship that has proved untenable. Divorce is the symptom, the final result, not the cause of a failed marriage. Divorced and not divorced, failed or successful, are merely results of the same institution of marriage. The calamitous effects of divorce on the family are not caused by the couple having divorced, but, in retrospect, by their having unwisely married to begin with, or not having committed on a more real, sensual level to making marriage work.

Children

If a couple parents its children well, it is not because the man and woman are married; it is because they are good parents. To the extent that they are mentally stable, mature, loving, or otherwise psychologically fit, parents will be good or bad parents, in or out of marriage.

Clearly, the breakup of couples has a very serious effect on most children, even if it does not force the wife and child into poverty. Undoubtedly, in many cases, children are better off if their parents break up. Nevertheless, on the whole and all other things being equal, the parental couple *living together* is clearly preferable for the emotional health and development of children.

A couple's breakup is usually more difficult for the children than for either parent. But couples seldom think about this before they get married. Premarital couples assume (for at least half of them it is a hallucination) that they will defy the odds and stay together as husband/father and wife/mother.

Some couples go further and expect that having children will help an already unhappy marriage, as if the additional roles of parents will help. In fact love was lost precisely because they were playing roles instead of being realistic with themselves and each other.

Above all, bad parenting, by teaching and example, whether associated with drug or alcohol abuse, the inability to bond intimately with their children, or any other emotional disorder, accounts for the poor adjustment of their children's personalities. It endangers the ability of those children to become stable spouses or parents, and establishes patterns so pervasive and unconscious that they shape society as a whole. This further affects each new generation in a self-perpetuating cycle of personality types and marital problems, one that has been handed down through history, largely by means of the institution of marriage.

As in other aspects of a mystical marriage, partners must be as conscious and open as they can be with regard to their expectations about children, child-rearing, and parental responsibility, even taking into account and discussing the possibility that their partnership could eventually break apart.

Mystical Marriage

In championing relationships based on spontaneous unity, the mystical traditions took a vastly different tack from that of the historical religiolegal marriage. Taoism, Tantrism, Gnosticism, Chivalry, Kabbalism, Alchemy, and later movements within the Enlightenment all promoted the freedom of the individual and women's equality. Van Gulik, for example, explained in his very lucid essay, "Chinese and Indian Sexual Mysticism":

> Tantrism, on the whole, enhanced the position of women in India, just as Taoism did in China. Contrary to traditional Hinduism, Tantrism considered women as equal to or even higher than man, and the Tantrists were among the early opponents of *suttee*, the burning of widows.
>   . . . Tantrism despised all religious and social traditions, it consciously trampled underfoot all the hallowed taboos. It refused to recognize the caste system and proclaimed woman to be the equal of man.

During the first centuries of the Christian era, in a practice roundly condemned by the church fathers, Gnostic men and women rebelled against the tyranny of marriage by openly living, sleeping, making love, and traveling together, but deliberately forgoing the formality of a religious or secular marriage. They considered themselves united instead by their actual feelings of love and mystical unity in what they called spiritual marriage. Rejecting the roles of husband and wife, they referred to themselves as spiritual brother and sister. By conscious design, these Gnostic couples were bonded, not by the arrangement of their parents, a governmental piece of paper, or the magic spell of a religious ritual, but by virtue of their feelings for each other, and their own decision as free individuals as to how they would relate with each other.

174

The contention that marriage is different from living to-gether because it helps a man and woman make a commitment to each other is baseless, as the identical internal commitments, sincere efforts, and statements of determinations to succeed forever as a couple can be made just as surely outside marriage as in it. Without a formal marriage, the man and woman are forced to recognize that their inner resources will bring about success or failure—not the wedding ceremony, or state licens-ing, or having been pronounced "husband and wife" by some-one else. Why shouldn't a woman and a man simply pronounce themselves married?

Marriage is a statement to the world, but a statement of what? Whatever a couple wants to state can be done so loudly and clearly, definitively, articulately, categorically, exquisitely, and completely, entirely outside marriage. The two can make a statement not only about love and commitment, but about re-spect, loyalty, honesty, sacrifice, personal growth, sharing, inti-macy, all of which can either exist or not exist inside or outside the sphere of marriage, as does sexual chemistry, emotional health, the accumulation of capital, bearing and raising chil-dren, and happiness in general.

Evolving toward a Mystical Marriage

Whether it's a legally formal relationship or not, mystical mar-riage is based on a couple's effort to know themselves and grow together. In order to know each other in a mystical marriage, a man and a woman strive to know themselves and each other through a process of introspection, communication, and per-sonal growth.

If you want to develop your relationship in the direction of mystical marriage, you can start by writing out in detail what you want from your partner and what you are willing to give.

Who should be more independent, active, powerful, controlling, compromising, dominant, loving, self-revealing, accepting, or understanding, and in what circumstances? How should you each approach or solve problems and handle disappointments and disagreements? List your sexual and personality and intelligence and moral expectations. How important are humor, hygiene, health, etiquette, appearance, monogamy, ambition, and outside interests?

Is there or should there be a division of labor? What specifically should that entail, with regard to money, children, love, recreation, and decisions in general? In what circumstances should you help each other, and what responsibility should be shared? How much will you talk with each other? Is there anything that shouldn't be discussed?

List and expand on all the other issues important to you in a relationship. While you're at it, try to identify how you came to hold your opinions on these topics. It is fascinating to explore how we arrive at our opinions and assumptions.

Then write out the histories of your significant past love relationships. What were their similarities? What patterns do they have in common with your present partnership? How did you happen to develop them? And sexually, what characteristics in a relationship are or were most erotic, exciting, and satisfying, in and out of bed? What was a turn-on to see, hear, and imagine, to do and have done?

Mysticism in marriage is concerned with the feelings, the emotional and tangible elements of a successful partnership, such as respect, kindness, intimacy, empathy, sexual chemistry, loyalty, even monogamy itself, and of course, love—feelings that have nothing in particular to do with marriage, per se. They are common to any intelligent, healthy human relationship, and are a matter of common sense and human nature, not tradition, religion, or marital law. They will be helpful to a male-female relationship or any other kind. Such human qualities have mainly to do with mental health and emotional adjustment. To think that they will suddenly come into play for two individuals simply by their marriage to each other is laughable.

It should be obvious that relationship problems are principally a result of the emotional problems of the individuals involved. But in fact many people think marital discord is caused by such symptomatic factors as sex or money problems. (One comedian joked that he and his wife are always arguing about sex and money—she charges him too much!)

The personal growth and autonomy of each lover as an individual is the best thing they can do for themselves *as a couple.* When a man and a woman approach their life partnership as a creative celebration of love and intimacy, there are no boundaries to the evolution of that couple's success and happiness, other than the personal limitations of the lovers themselves as individuals.

How does one overcome one's personal limitations? Of course, this is a global question about mental health, personal growth, and the human soul, about which whole libraries have been written, and all without a final word. We can only try to sketch a sample of preliminary steps to personal growth. These steps can be taken as a preparation for a relationship or as a part of a process to make an ongoing relationship more real.

Just to begin with, sit and think about your disappointments, shortcomings, fears, failings, sources of frustration and anger and other negative feelings, deepest secrets, most embarrassing problems, and the areas in need of work and improvement. Also think about your goals, strengths, sources of joy and happiness and fulfillment and contentedness, expectations from life, love, and a family, and a nation, and the cosmos. Write it all down. Begin a diary with your life history, your whole life, beginning with your childhood and adolescence, your parents, their patterns of relating with each other, and with you and your siblings. For instance, how did they show love and discipline you? And how are your brothers and sisters doing now? Write out your experiences with religion, arts, hobbies, sports, exercise, employment, and school; social groups and individual friends of each sex, before and after puberty; your health, growth; experiences with drugs and alcohol (your own and those of significant others); your feelings about your body, and about yourself as a person.

Once you begin to analyze your own background, do some reading on related subjects, attend lectures and self-help groups. Speak with friends, a therapist or other counselor, and above all with your partner. Spend as much time on it as on hobbies, recreation, and TV. Make it an ongoing, major project, a life's work. Do you have no personal problems? Are they all someone else's fault? Your partner's fault? *Definitely* see a therapist. With or without professional help, begin to work, to grow, to begin to evolve as a person. This is why, properly gone about, marriage is hard work.

One major function of psychotherapy is to enable an individual to admit to another person, but especially to oneself, the innermost secrets and personal sensitivities one hides from others (and just as often from oneself). This is an important function, but therapy should not be used to diffuse the need to confide in one's partner.

Communicate with your partner what you are learning about yourself. What will your partner think? What will your partner do? What will you think and do as you begin to learn more about your partner?

Sometimes it's easier just to get married. Often the act of getting married is a cover-up for a lack of total honesty. If we're married, we won't have to deal with the secrets, fears, of rejection, doubts, and expectations of the other, or of oneself, we believe. But such beliefs inhibit personal growth. Personal growth is the ongoing education and experience of oneself in order to evolve toward a harmony, a balance, a coordination of the aspects of one's inner self, and of one's relationship with the outer world—a balance of feeling and knowing, of discipline and spontaneity, of love and autonomy, of celebration and sacrifice, of self and other, I and Thou. It is indeed hard work, a life's work, the Great Work. To know thyself, and thy partner. But this ongoing positive change is how one keeps the monogamous from becoming the monotonous.

Self-awareness exercises like these are a good place to start, but don't limit yourself to these few questions. Of course, there are no right or wrong answers. The important thing is that one is in touch with oneself and one's expectations, and begins to express and discuss them with one's partner or potential partner. It is that openness which allows lovers to really know each other, instead of relating to an image or fantasy or unconscious assumption about each other.

Mysticism and Verbal Communication

Mysticism offers some insights into how couples can best communicate with each other. Perhaps the single most important guideline for effective interpersonal communication is to speak in terms of right hemisphere consciousness. From that approach one speaks in terms of one's own opinion, point of view, taste and perspective, feelings, preferences, likes or dislikes, expectations, and what one wants, rather than labeling, name-calling, evaluating, theorizing, moralizing, classifying, and other cognitive-conceptual left-brain analyses. Surely it is not coincidental that "feeling talk" is the most widely recommended communication advice given by marriage counselors today, and is one of the bases for the dozens of fine self-help books on assertiveness training that appeared in the mid-1970s during the heyday of behavior therapy.

To speak in terms of right hemisphere consciousness is not

simply a sentimental nicety. Modern philosopher Charles Stevenson, in his very convincing *Ethics and Language*, demonstrated how, "This is good, that is bad," logically means merely, "I like this, I disapprove of that; and I want you to agree with me!" This is why intuition and compassion, being in touch with one's own and one's partner's inner feelings, are not only the keys to mysticism's approach to morality, but to good verbal communication in an intimate partnership.

Communicating on the right side of the mind goes hand in hand with a mystical philosophy of human relations, which suggests that partners act toward each other spontaneously, according to their intuitive feelings, inner compassion, and human heartedness, rather than according to externally imposed ethical guidelines. This is why mysticism does not engage in moralizing or setting out specific rules of right and wrong behavior.

Tantrism, according to Bharati, "is more value-free than non-tantric traditions; moralizing, and other be-good clichés, are set aside." "Morally, Taoist philosophy is completely indifferent," explains Herrlee Creel. "All things are relative. 'Right' and 'wrong' are just words which we may apply to the same thing, depending upon which partial viewpoint we see it from." Walker tells us that Gnosis "has nothing to do with morality. . . . Laws, religious, moral, and social, are of little relevance."

That ethics is not fixed but involves a sense of feel and taste was addressed by the philosopher Ludwig Wittgenstein in his classic *Tractatus Logico-Philosophicus*:

> 6.4.2 . . . it is impossible for there to be propositions of ethics.
> 6.4.21 . . . ethics cannot be put into words. Ethics is transcendental. (Ethics and aesthetics are one and the same.)

That ethics cannot be put into words, but is properly a matter of feeling and compassion, is the underlying philosophical reason we cannot spell out the rules of a mystical marriage. Instead of fixed, external rules and roles that the various moralities say couples should adhere to, mysticism recommends that lovers trust their own internal sense of loving compassion and empathy to guide their behavior toward each other.

Morality, on the other hand, involves the affixing of abstract, emotionally charged words such as "good, evil, right, wrong, fair, and unfair" to actions that are approved or disapproved of by whoever is using this tactic. Such ethical terms can be categorized as persuasive definitions, and are very powerfully, emotionally valenced. Hence, they constantly pop up in political rhetoric, sales, and other smarmy practices, in addition to being a major technique of mass population control employed by all the imperial theologies. Morality is one example of how popular theology seeks to promote a left hemisphere consciousness, as does hypnosis, because the more that people are operating on the level of words, the more they are vulnerable to verbal suggestion and instructions. This is why all popular religion involves an endless amount of verbal repetition and disapproves morally of right-brain or altered consciousness, prohibiting to one degree or another, music, dancing, drinking, other sensual endeavors, and, above all, sex.

But "good" and "evil" have no intrinsic meaning whatsoever; they are entirely relativistic, changing according to the aims, values, and motivations of the people employing them. In fact, as they are entirely conceptual, they don't even *exist* except as notions in the imagination of the left brain. One cannot have a bucket of goodness or a bag of evil.

Of course, mysticism's rejection of moralizing must not be confused with compulsive or bizarre or anarchic license for lovers or anyone else. Nor is it a suggestion that we abandon law and order. Perhaps it is time, however, to abandon our naïve reliance on laws and morals as keys to creating civil, brotherly love, or successful marriages. Furthermore, not only do most people not need moralizing, those who do "need" it are precisely the ones who won't use it. The most disturbed individuals either ignore all sense of compassion and social consciousness, or use morality as a cover-up for obsessive mental rigidity, a codependent personality, or other emotional illness. This is why the road to hell is so often paved with good, moral intentions, in and out of a love partnership. Left-brain, moral evaluations do not keep us on the loving path. They divert us from knowing and trusting the natural human compassion within our hearts.

Nor can communication technique be perfectly spelled out, any more than sex technique can be. But it can indeed be useful to be involved in an ongoing search for helpful hints and suggestions that are meaningful for the individual and the couple. For example, virtually all of the assertiveness literature recommends responsive listening. This means giving full attention, physically and emotionally, using good eye contact, nodding, leaning forward and letting the speaker know you're listening and understanding by feeding back the message, and especially the feelings behind the message. And above all, it involves being aware of the feelings brought about within you in response to your partner, and trying to understand what it is about you that caused you to react emotionally in the way you did—then trying to express those feelings and discoveries to your partner.

Monogamy

Mysticism encourages the monogamous unity and partnership of a man and a woman as equal halves of a spiritual and physical unity, not only in mystical sex, but in a shared lifetime together. One cannot specify what to do in a mystical marriage, because a mystical marriage implies an attitude, a spontaneous state of mind in which the partners do not play fixed roles.

Just as couples will stay together without the institution of marriage, so spouses will act and feel and behave just as lovingly without religious commandments or roles that tradition says a husband and wife should play. Instead they can sense each other as human beings, and spontaneously act and react to each other in a continuous flow of feelings. Couples can act more compassionately, more intelligently, and lovingly, even at times heroically, if they behave according to their own feelings, rather than if they are mechanically acting according to externally imposed ethics.

Not that a mystical way of relating is easy because there are no moral rules. It means nearly the reverse—a totally new attitude in approaching a love relationship, in which one is vulnerable enough to reveal oneself fully, and compassionate enough to understand and respect a partner's inner experience. Far from easy, it takes courage and a sense of adventure to be open and vulnerable with one's feelings and to have the strength to tolerate, metabolize, and accept a partner's honesty and candor.

In his classic, *Nature, Man and Woman*, Alan Watts explored how "spontaneity, after all, is total sincerity." In this way, spontaneity in a mystical marriage involves a man and a woman relating to each other honestly, as the individuals they actually are, rather than according to roles or conceptual preprogrammed images of themselves and each other, as we have described them.

The Role of Mystical Sex

Whether or not mystical sex is part of a cure for our culture's erotification of misogyny, and while it is hardly necessary for a successful relationship, the benefits that it can and does provide for many couples is significant. It may be something of a miracle for those couples who have a problem in the sexual area of their relationship; their dysphoria over such problems is frequently indescribable, as ineffable in a negative sense as mystical sex is positive. Even for those couples who have a good love life, mystical sex is the sharing of a closeness, a timeless unity, a real unhurried physical intimacy, and a peak emotional experience that bonds partners more closely each time they make love.

Mystical sex provides a freedom from stress and tension, both physically and emotionally. It allows for forgiveness and a healing rejuvenation of fondness and love between partners. The experience of mystical sex is a break, a respite, from the rat race of the workaday world into which a man and a woman venture alone each day. It is an arrival at the source of tranquility and recuperation, a recharging of each other's emotional batteries, a place to come back to, a return to the paradise that is lost when lovers separate, a mutual elevation to the bliss, the peace from which there is nowhere else to go. You're there, you've arrived, and you're off on an ecstatic flight above and beyond the concepts of mind and body.

Mystical sex can be part of a healing process on both emotional and physical levels—for mysticism they are the same—because of the vital human need for closeness, touching, and affection. This need is not orgasmic or even sexual; it is the need for the physical intimacy of holding and being held closely, gently, lovingly, which is with us from infancy through old age.

In one of modern psychology's classic laboratory experiments, Dr. Harry Harlow showed that when baby rhesus monkeys were given adequate food and shelter, but were deprived of physical affection, they grew up exhibiting humanlike emotional disorders, including a schizoid difficulty in socializing with normally raised monkeys. This points not only to the cause of some human mental illness, but to the way such disorders can be passed from generation to generation: emotionally and affectionally unavailable parents can cause the same disorder to arise in their infants, who later cannot emotionally nourish their children. This need for intimacy, combined with how badly many husbands make love, may be why a majority of women surveyed would rather be held lovingly than engage in "the act." Fortunately, mystical sex offers both kinds of contact at once, and so much more that it cannot help but help the monogamous unity of any loving couple.

Dr. Andrew Weil has asserted that it is also a natural human need to experience altered states of consciousness, the inappropriate expression of which translates into the drug and alcohol abuse problem epidemic in our culture. This crisis is implicated in an enormous number of failed marriages today, primarily because such chronic misuse of drugs prevents the experience of intimacy in general and the mystical unity of partners in particular. Perhaps the altered states of consciousness brought about during mystical sex will be a healthy fulfillment of the need for those states now self-abusively brought about by drugs and alcohol—and thereby part of a solution to our tragic problems of addiction and substance abuse.

Incidentally, the mystical traditions were not opposed to drugs and alcohol. Bacchus was the god of beer and wine, and drunkenness was regarded as the direct perception of and transsubstantial unity with the wine, and thereby the divine. But such use of wine and other drugs was reserved for specially guided initiatory and educational occasions, as an aid to perception, insight, and understanding of oneself and the cosmos. This was a far cry from today's spastic and bizarre misuse of alcohol and drugs in which mind-altering substances are compulsively ingested as an avoidance of life, a delusion and dulling of the senses, and an unconsciously paranoid flight from connections with people and reality—precisely the opposite method and purpose for drug use recommended by the mystical traditions.

✦ ✦ ✦

Mystical sex, lovemaking that causes an altered state of mind or mystical experience, was the approach to sex recommended by all the mystical traditions, those religions that emphasized a right-brain hemisphere consciousness, and an attitude of celebration, chivalry, and creativity toward life. While mysticism rejected marriage as a concept and an institution, it simultaneously embraced the monogamous unity of a man and a woman as their most natural state of being.

I hope that in reading this book you have seen that mysticism is not so strange, not so weird, not so mysterious. And that mystical sex is not so elusive, unusual, or difficult to experience, occurring entirely without magic and make-believe, pompous moralities and meditations, or promises of a greater, future reward way off in a distant place and time. Maybe if mystical sex gives us anything, it is the realization that the fulfillment of a natural unity with the cosmos is at our fingertips. It is a question of attitude, a state of mind, a knowledge based on feeling—and based on an acceptance of that feeling and thereby of reality, of life, and of oneself, a simple separate person.

"What have you done with your gift of sex?" asked Kafka. "It was a failure, in the end that is all they will say. But it might easily have succeeded. A mere trifle, indeed so small as not to be perceived, decided between its failure and success." It is hoped that this book may have been that trifle for you, an insight that made that difference between failure and success, or between mere success and the fulfillment of a lifetime.

Bibliography

Adams, Blanche, et al. *Woman, Assert Yourself!* New York: Harper and Row, 1974.

Alberti, Robert, and Michael Emmons. *Stand Up, Speak Out, Talk Back!* New York: Pocket Books, 1975.

Alberti, Robert, and Michael Emmons. *Your Perfect Right.* San Luis Obispo, Calif.: Impact, 1970.

Allen, Woody. *Woody Allen, Volume 2.* New York: Colpix Records, 1965.

American Psychiatric Association. *Diagnostic and Statistical Manual of Mental Disorders.* Washington, D.C.: APA, 1987.

Annon, Jack. *The Behavioral Treatment of Sexual Problems.* Honolulu: Enabling Systems, 1974.

Aycock, Lay. "Medical Management of Premature Ejaculation," *Journal of Urology* 2 (September 1949).

Baer, Jean. *How to Be an Assertive (Not Aggressive) Woman.* New York: Signet, 1976.

Balzac, Honoré de. *The Physiology of Marriage.* New York: Liveright, 1932.

Barahti, Agehananda. *The Tantric Tradition.* New York: Samuel Weiser, 1965.

Bension, Ariel. *The Zohar.* London: George Routledge and Sons, 1932.

Bhattacharyya, N.N. *History of the Tantric Tradition.* New Delhi: Manohar, 1982.

Bloom, Lynn, et al. *The New Assertive Woman.* New York: Dell, 1975.

Brecker, Edward, and Jeremy Brecker. "Sex Is Good for Your Health," *Playboy* (January 1976).

Briggs, George, trans. *Goraknatha and the Kanphata Yogis.* Calcutta: n.p., 1938.

Brown, Spencer. *Laws of Form.* New York: Julian Press, 1972.

Burton, Sir Richard. *The Kama Sutra of Vatsayana.* New York: G.P. Putnam, 1963.

Burton, Sir Richard. *Perfumed Garden.* New York: G.P. Putnam, 1964.

Byron, Lord George. *Don Juan.* New York: Heritage, 1943.

Campbell, Joseph. *The Power of Myth.* New York: Doubleday, 1988.

Capra, Fritjof. *The Tao of Physics.* Berkeley: Shambala, 1975.

Chang, Jolan. *The Tao of Love and Sex.* New York: E.P. Dutton, 1977.

Cohen, Alan, et al. "EEG Hemispheric Asymmetry during Sexual Arousal," *Journal of Abnormal Psychology* 94:4 (1985).

Creel, Herrlee. *What Is Taoism?* Chicago: University of Chicago Press, 1970.

Csikszentmihalyi, Mihaly. *Flow: The Psychology of Optimal Experience.* New York: Harper and Row, 1990.

Daniélou, Alain. *Shiva and Dionysus.* K.F. Hurry, trans. London and the Hague: East-West Publications, 1982.

Dantzig, Tobias. *Number: The Language of Science.* New York: Free Press, 1954.

Dasgupta, S.B. *Introduction to Tantric Buddhism.* Calcutta: University of Calcutta Press, 1974.

Dickinson, R.L., and Louise Bryant. *The Control of Conception.* Baltimore: Williams and Wilkins, 1931.

Dickinson, R.L. *A Thousand Marriages.* Baltimore: Williams and Wilkins, 1931.

Dodds, E.R. *Euripides' Bacchae.* Oxford: Clarendon Press, 1960.

Douglas, Nik. *Tantra Yoga.* New Delhi: Manoharcal, 1970.

Dowling, Collette. *The Cinderella Complex.* New York: Pocket Books, 1988.

Dwyer, William. *What Everyone Knew about Sex, Explained in the Words of Orson Squire Fowler and Other Victorian Moralists.* Princeton: Pyne Press, 1972.

Edwards, Betty. *Drawing on the Right Side of the Brain.* Los Angeles: Tarcher, 1979.

Eliade, Mircea. *The Forge and the Crucible*. Chicago: University of Chicago Press, 1978.

Eliade, Mircea. *History of Religious Beliefs*, vols. 1 and 2. Chicago: University of Chicago Press, 1978/82.

Eliade, Mircea. *Mephistopheles and the Adrogyne*. New York: Sheed and Ward, 1965.

Eliade, Mircea. *Techniques du Yoga*. Paris: Gallimard, 1975.

Eliade, Mircea. *Yoga: Immortality and Freedom*. Princeton: Princeton University Press, 1958.

Evans, Arthur. *God of Ecstasy*. New York: St. Martin's Press, 1988.

Evola, Julius. *Metaphysics of Sex*. New York: Inner Traditions, 1983.

Farrell, Warren. *Why Men Are the Way They Are*. New York: McGraw-Hill, 1986.

Fasteau, Marc. *Male Machine*. New York: Delta, 1975.

Fensterheim, Herbert, and Jean Baer. *Don't Say Yes When You Want To Say No*. New York: Dell, 1975.

Fisher, Seymour. *Female Orgasm*. New York: Allen Lane, 1973.

Fox, Matthew. *Coming of the Cosmic Christ*. San Francisco: Harper and Row, 1988.

Fromm, Erich. *The Art of Loving*. New York: Harper and Row, 1962.

Fuller, Buckminster. *Synergetics*. New York: Macmillan, 1973.

Gonzalez-Wippler, Migene. *Kabbalah for the Modern World*. St. Paul: Llewellyn, 1987.

Haley, Jay. *Strategies of Psychotherapy*. New York: Grune and Stratton, 1963.

Hansen, Eric. *Stranger in the Forest*. Boston: Houghton Mifflin, 1988.

Harlow, Harry. *From Learning to Love*. New York: Praeger, 1986.

Hartman, William, and Marilyn Fithian. *Treatment of Sexual Dysfunction*. Long Beach: Center for Marital and Sexual Studies, 1972.

Hirsch, Edwin. *Power to Love*. New York: Citadel, 1939.

Huizinga, J. *Waning of the Middle Ages*. London: Bulter and Tanner, 1924.

James, William. *Varieties of Religious Experience.* New York: Mentor, 1958.

Kaplan, Helen Singer. *Disorders of Sexual Desire.* New York: Simon and Schuster, 1979.

Kaplan, Helen Singer. *New Sex Therapy.* New York: Brunner/Mazel, 1974.

Kinsey, Alfred, et al. *Sexual Behavior in the Human Male.* Philadelphia: W.B. Saunders, 1948.

Kotin, J., et al. "Thioridizine and Sexual Dysfunction," *American Journal of Psychiatry* 133:1 (January 1976).

Krafft-Ebing, Richard von. *Psychopathia Sexualis.* New York: Physicians and Surgeons, 1906.

Kramer, Heinrich, and James Sprenger. *Malleus Maleficarum.* M. Summers, trans. New York: Dover, 1971.

Lawlor, Robert. *Sacred Geometry.* New York: Crossroads, 1982.

Lawrence, D.H. *Lady Chatterly's Lover.* New York: Bantam, 1968.

Leibowitz, Michael. *The Chemistry of Love.* Boston: Little, Brown, 1983.

Levine, Steven. "Barriers to the Attainment of Ejaculatory Control," *Medical Aspects of Human Sexuality* 13:1 (January 1979).

Levy, Howard, and Ishihara, Akira. *Tao of Sex.* New York: Harper and Row, 1968.

Lowen, Alexander. *Love and Orgasm.* New York: Collier, 1965.

MacKinnon, Catherine. *Feminism Unmodified.* Cambridge: Harvard University Press, 1987.

Maslow, Abraham. *Religions, Values, and Peak Experiences.* Columbus: Ohio State University Press, 1964.

Maspéro, Henri. "Les Procédés de 'Nourir l'Esprit Vital' dans la Religion Taoíste Ancienne," *Journal Asiatique* 229 (April-June, July-September 1937).

Maspéro, Henri. *Le Taoísm.* Paris: Gallimard, 1971.

Masters, William, and Virginia Johnson. *Human Sexual Inadequacy.* Boston: Little, Brown, 1970.

Masters, William, and Virginia Johnson. *Human Sexual Response*. Boston: Little, Brown, 1966.

Maugham, W. Somerset. *The Summing Up*. New York: Doubleday Doran, 1939.

Meldman, Louis. *Modification of Male Sexual Behavior*. Ann Arbor: Xerox University Microfilms, 1981.

Meldman, Monte. *Diseases of Attention and Perception*. London: Pergamon Press, 1970.

Meyer, Marvin. *The Ancient Mysteries*. San Francisco: Harper and Row, 1987.

Mill, John Stuart. *On the Subjugation of Women*. Cambridge: MIT Press, 1970.

Miller, George, et al. *Plans in the Structure of Behavior*. New York: Holt, Rinehart and Winston, 1960.

Miller, Henry. *Tropic of Cancer*. New York: Grove, 1961.

Money, John, and Herman Musaph. *Handbook of Sexology*. New York: Excerpta Medica, 1977.

Nelli, René. *L'Erotique des Troubadors*. Paris: E. Privat, 1984.

Nietzsche, Friedrich. *Beyond Good and Evil*. Helen Zimmern, trans. London: Allen and Unwin, 1967.

Noyes, John Humphrey. *Male Continence*. New York: Office of the Onieda Circular, 1872.

O'Donohugh, Bernard. *The Courtly Love Tradition*. Manchester: Manchester University Press, 1982.

Paz, Octavio. *Sunstone: Collected Poems of Octavio Paz, 1957–1987*. Elliot Weinberg, ed. and trans. New York: New Directions, 1987.

Peck, M. Scott. *The Road Less Traveled*. New York: Touchstone, 1978.

Phelps, Stanlee, and Nancy Austin. *The Assertive Woman*. San Luis Obispo, Calif.: Impact, 1975.

Polya, G. *How to Solve It*. Princeton: Princeton University Press, 1945.

Prabhupada, A.C. *The Bagavad-Gita, As It Is*. New York: Collier, 1972.

Rawson, Philip. *Tantra.* London: Thames and Hudson, 1973.

Reich, Wilhelm. *Function of the Orgasm.* T. Wolfe, trans. New York: Noonday, 1942.

Reiff, Philip. *Freud: The Mind of the Moralist.* Chicago: University of Chicago Press, 1959.

Rola, S.K. de. *Alchemy.* London: Thames and Hudson, 1973.

Rougemont, Denis de. *Love in the Western World.* New York: Pantheon Books, 1956.

Russell, Bertrand. *History of Western Philosophy.* New York: Touchstone, 1945.

Saint Augustine. *City of God.* M. Dods, trans. Edinburgh: Clark, 1872.

Sanger, Margaret. *Magnetation Methods of Birth Control.* N. P., 1915.

Semans, James. "Premature Ejaculation: A New Approach," *Southern Medical Journal* 49 (April 1956).

Singer, June. *Androgeny.* Garden City, N.Y.: Anchor/Doubleday, 1967.

Singer, June. *Energies of Love.* Garden City, N.Y.: Anchor/Doubleday, 1983.

Smith, Manuel. *When I Say No I Feel Guilty.* New York: Dial Press, 1975.

Stekel, Wilhelm. "Psychology of Premature Ejaculation," *Disorders of Instincts and Emotions.* New York: Liveright, 1927.

Stendhal. *On Love.* New York: Liveright, 1947.

Stevenson, Charles. *Ethics and Language.* New Haven: Yale University Press, 1944.

Sun Tzu. *The Art of War.* S.B. Griffith, trans. Oxford: Oxford University Press, 1963.

Szasz, Thomas. *Myth of Psychotherapy.* New York: Doubleday, 1978.

Szasz, Thomas. *Sex by Prescription.* New York: Anchor/Doubleday, 1980.

Taubman, Byrna. *How to Become an Assertive Woman.* New York: Pocket Books, 1976.

Thurber, James. *Men, Women and Dogs.* New York: Dodd, Mead, 1975.

Thurin, Erik. *Emerson as Priest of Pan.* Lawrence: Regents of Kansas, 1981.

Vandenbroek, Andre. *Philosophical Geometry.* Rochester, Vt.: Inner Traditions, 1972.

van de Veldt, T. *Ideal Marriage.* New York: Random House, 1927.

Von Urban, Rudolf. *Sex Perfection and Marital Happiness.* New York: Dial, 1949.

Waite, A.E. *Holy Kabbalah.* Secaucus, N.J.: University Books, 1960.

Walker, Benjamin. *Gnosticism.* Wellington, Northhamptonshire: Aquarian Books, 1983.

Walker, Kenneth, and Eric Strauss. *Sexual Disorders in the Male.* Baltimore: Williams and Wilkins, 1939.

Watts, Alan. *In My Own Way.* New York: Vintage, 1973.

Watts, Alan. *Nature, Man and Woman.* New York: Pantheon Books, 1958.

Watts, Alan. *Psychotherapy East and West.* New York: Ballantine, 1961.

Weil, Andrew. *The Natural Mind.* Boston: Houghton Mifflin, 1972.

White, John. "Kundalini: Sex, Evolution and Higher Consciousness," *Spiritual India and Kundalini* 1 (October-December 1977).

Whitman, Walt. *One's Self I Sing.* In *English Poetry,* Charles Eliot, ed. New York: P.F. Collier, 1938.

Wittgenstein, Ludwig. *Tractatus Logico-Philosophicus.* Pears and McGinness, trans. London: Routledge and Kegan Paul, 1961.